Wait For It:

Walking In FAITH

———————

Aurora Lynn Dubell Newton

Wait For It: Walking In FAITH

ISBN: 978-1511679633

Dedication

This book is dedicated first to God, my Heavenly Daddy, who has seen me through every journey! Without the new challenge in my life, this book would have never happened. I love you and will trust you into eternity. Second it is dedicated to Pop, my earthly Daddy. The last 14 years of my life have been so rich thanks to your friendship and love. You have truly shown the love of God the Father through the way you love your children. The world and my life is a better place because of you! Thank you for all the years you sacrificed to raise me, provided for me, and your continued prayers for all of us!!

Acknowledgments

Originally I listed dozens of people and organizations in my acknowledgements. I felt compelled in this update to take out all of the names. A prompting from the Holy Spirit said that I needed to keep it simple. Therefore I share that if you know me; I acknowledge you have had a profound impact in my life in one way or another. If you do not know me but are a powerful man or woman of God in the world, I am sure I have studied your teachings, listened to a sermon, watched a video, or tuned into a radio or television program and have been greatly impacted. I acknowledge that we can do nothing apart from Christ if we claim to be Christians so therefore I acknowledge Christ in you and say thank you for saying yes to being used to impact the world particularly my world.

Much Love and Thanks

Scott, my beloved husband. You were such a surprise when I believed I would be a single mom for the rest of my life. Your love, steadfastness, and sensitivity in giving me the freedom to be who God has called me to be are a most treasured gift! Thank you for all your edits! I appreciate the time sacrificed to see this book birthed!

Matt, I am so proud of the man of God you are and your commitment to trust Him in your life. You are a rare and special person. I thank you for the hours and hours you spent worshipping and praying with me! Your heart to "Not conform to the pattern of this world" is a sacrificial lifestyle that the Lord continues to honor in you! You are one of my best friends and I love you son!

Clint, there are very few people I have found in this life with your sense of loyalty. You love people with such a passion like Christ. I am blessed by the way you are following God in your life. You have taught me so much about myself! I love our lunch dates! I love you son!

My Extended Family – My bro's, Robbie, Danny, and Stevie, my sister in laws (I really consider them my sisters), Kathy and Helain, my nieces, Jill, Christina, Sherri, Julie, Katie, Krissa, Megan, Leah, and my nephews, Bobby, Steven, Michael, Scotty… thanks for your encouragement and support. I love you all! My nephew in laws Mitch and Eric – love you guys so much!

Kari Sowder – WOW girl – you are always there encouraging, directing, and just plain doing life with me. Thanks for your edits and input. I look forward to many more book journeys with you!

Karey Akers – I so appreciate your honesty and friendship! Some of the best edits in this book were because you took the risk and spoke truth in love! Thank you!!

Forward

His smile. His gaze. I have wondered so many times what it would have been like to look into Jesus' profoundly loving eyes, to stare intensely without looking away, to receive what is exuded. I remember in Luke 7 the beautiful story of a sinful woman who anointed Jesus. The scriptures say in v.37,

"When a woman who had lived a sinful life in that town learned that Jesus was eating at the Pharisee's house, she brought an alabaster jar of perfume,..."

The interesting part is that she obviously had heard of Jesus. Her first encounter with Him must have been so disorientating. He was so drastically different. She didn't know how to process the depth of the His love. I envision her later accosting people as she frantically searched up alleys and backstreets asking everyone if they had seen Jesus. How I wish I knew more of her first interaction with Him that would lead her to worship Him publicly without fear of the humiliation and shame that would be projected upon her.

My dear friend, Aurora Newton, is one of the most anointed people I have ever met. The depth and power of her love are absolutely disorienting. Like the sinful woman's encounter with Jesus, experiencing that deep gaze and love of Aurora entices a person to want to know the Savior more. It entices a person to worship Him with their all.

Leaders are known for a myriad of reasons. The list of leadership gifts, traits and attributes is exhausting, but the most important leadership trait is love. Aurora's love is without comparison.

When Judas' position as an apostle was being replaced, the prayer in Acts 1:24 & 25 says,

5

"Lord, you know everyone's heart (emphasis added). Show us which of these two you have chosen to take over this apostolic ministry, which Judas left to go where he belongs."

Clearly, what mattered most was the heart of the next apostle! What matters most?!? The heart! Aurora abounds in wisdom and anointing... but her heart is radiant beyond words.

She is a woman who is unmoved by circumstances. Her articulated theology (what she says she believes) matches her functional theology (what her life says she believes).

When you are with her, it's like she is from another realm. She is living as if she has received all that she's hoping for even though in many ways she's still "waiting for it."

Adam Vaughan
Pastor, Missionary, Friend
www.thebackwardsmissionaries.com
avaughanfam@gmail.com

CONTENTS

INTRODUCTION

(MUST READ TO UNDERSTAND CHAPTER 1)

We live in a world that does not like to wait for anything. Much of what we do happens within minutes and sometimes seconds after we request it. I have had someone text me and then within minutes of me not responding, text me again asking why I have not responded. I have chuckled at times and thought, "Do I really have to answer a text while trying to go to the bathroom"? But let's face it; it has come down to that for many people. I have been that one waiting for it, expecting it almost instantaneously. In our world of rush and hurry, we rarely have patience to wait, yet **I have found it is in the waiting and hoping that the most beautiful stories have unfolded**. It is in the waiting that this journey begins and will ultimately end. It started with a medical diagnosis, and continues after the ending of this book, as I WAIT FOR IT…, the confirmation of healing! I want to begin with a story of asking and waiting for something from God that may seem superficial or "not spiritual", but for me it is all spiritual. This story shows the depth with which God desires intimate relationship with us and answers our prayers!

Recently, our son Matt came to us and said that he wanted to propose to his girlfriend. He is in fulltime ministry with very little pay so there was no extra money for a ring. We did what we usually do and asked the Lord to provide the finances for him to afford a ring. We also prayed that we would trust God's timing and not rush the engagement without the ring. We asked Matt to be patient and WAIT FOR IT, the answer. He committed his life to the Lord at a very early age and has spent much of his time waiting yet still walking in the promises and prophetic words to be fully birthed in his life. Likewise, he was committed to WAIT FOR IT, God's timing and provision of the finances to buy a ring to propose to his girlfriend. I do not suggest that waiting on the Lord means to sit around and do nothing. I believe that we need to be active not idle, walking out our life in faith. However, we also need to exercise patience in the waiting for prayers to be answered. If we can achieve it on our own it may not be God sized. It's too easy to act instead of pause and wait for what we could not possibly accomplish on our own.

At times I have seen prayers answered immediately like the healing of sight. Sometimes you have to WAIT FOR IT, the answer, but I assure you God does answer! Sometimes it may not be what we want to hear or the way we want to hear it but it comes! That's really the sum of this book, this journey; it is in believing and choosing to see God in all aspects of life. It's not easy or for the faint of heart. It has taken a long time for me to be able to come to a place where I can keep walking while I am waiting and dreaming. In fact, I had to navigate through a lot of hurt, pain, and offense in my life to finally realize that I needed to **let go of my offense and let God be my defense**. It is only in the letting go of the past that we can find peace in the present and joy to press into the future. This journey you are about to take with me comes from a lifetime of walking from tragedy to triumph, refusing to grow bitter but pressing on, standing and choosing to WAIT FOR IT, God's best as I walk in faith. I believe that through reading my journey, you may see the hope in your own journey and find the strength to WAIT FOR IT, God's answer. I hope that these pages inspire and encourage you! They have encouraged me as I typed them and reflected!

Chapter 1

ONE RINGY DINGY

Okay, so I will not make you "WAIT FOR IT" long. The ring, I am talking about waiting for the rest of the ring story, when we prayed for the engagement ring. This is a story that I still can barely believe but it is true. Shortly after we prayed for provision to purchase a ring, now mind you, I was thinking a couple hundred dollars and hopefully several months away. Anyway, a very dear friend came to me to tell me that she had a sense from the Lord that she was supposed to give an engagement ring to Matt to propose to his girlfriend.

WHAT, ARE YOU KIDDING ME - SERIOUSLY?

We told **NO ONE** about our prayer which happened in the dawn of the morning as we welcomed the day and Matt and I shared a cup of coffee together. Matt and Nicke had not been dating long so when he came to us about wanting to propose, we all felt that the timing would be, at the minimum, months away.

This story, like most stories in our lives, can be traced back to other events that have unfolded, painting a picture of a long and winding road, which brings us to the current moment. This is one such story. If I just ended it where we are right now it would be fantastic. We prayed, a ring was provided. However, in the true nature of God, it is a story that only He could knit together. It is important to point out that anywhere along the way; the story would have changed if each person did not respond when they heard from the Lord. Obedience to His voice is so very important. The Bible states in John 10:27, "**My sheep listen to my voice; I know them, and they follow me**." Listening to His voice will change the course of a journey and a story.

Several years back, as a single mom, I was determined to be the best mom I could be. The question was, "Where does that begin"? For me, I knew it was rooted in my identity. Being a mom was a job but being a daughter of King Jesus was who I really was (and am). I decided to commit my life to becoming the best "bride of Christ" I could be. I had no clue what that even meant at the time but I was determined! I dug my heels in and contemplated where to begin. Oh yes, a ring. Isn't that the symbol that binds a marriage the never ending circle? So with what little money I had extra, I went out and purchased a beautiful white gold and diamond ring to seal my commitment. I focused on growing from bitter in my circumstances to better in my walk with God.

After three years of this commitment, the Lord brought my husband Scott into my life. This was another amazing story of God's grace. I was not expecting or waiting for another man in my life. Not that I hated men, I just knew that I need to be healthy and whole for myself and my children and, relationally, that had not been where I was. I was content walking with God and raising my sons. However, God had a different plan. Scott and I were not in a season of financial abundance when we met. In fact, when we talked about getting married, he shared that he could not afford a ring to propose to me. I told him I did not care. He was amazing and I already had a ring I loved, so we could use that as an engagement ring. We had committed ourselves to purity in our relationship and he wanted to do things the "old fashioned way" so he took the ring and decided to propose when he felt the time was right. He also wanted to ask my dad for his approval. This was all very new to me. I had not waited for anything in my past relationships so I truly loved what was unfolding! I was scheduled to go on a mission trip that summer to India with a team of teens and adults. Matt, who was 12 years old at that time, was also going. Scott proposed beforehand and the wedding was set for a little over a month after we arrived home from India. This story is so exciting I can hardly wait to type it all out for you to read. I wish you could hear the excitement in my voice as it spills forth. Alas, in the true nature of this book, you are going to have to be patient and wait for it as you read the whole story as it unfolds.

As we disembarked from the plane in India, armed guards manned posts throughout the airport. After a 22 hour plane stay (we had a layover in Europe and could not get off of the plane) we made our way to retrieve 44 luggage bags. We had 22 on our team and took the limit of suitcases so that we could bring crafts and things for the children we would be teaching! The guards smiled and responded to my smiles and greetings of excitement and enthusiasm with a cheerful, "Welcome". I have found that throughout my worldly travel, even the toughest looking and acting people respond pretty much how they are treated. The armed guards did not stifle the anticipation of all that was waiting for us. India had a plethora of sights, sounds, and smells that were new and appealing to different senses. As we left the airport, two huge dump truck looking vehicles awaited and our 44 bags were tossed into the back by our rugged hosts. As we drove through the dirt covered roads on our way to the hotel, naked children were asleep on the sides of the road. There were some who had cardboard homes but many lay uncovered as the sun slowly began to appear in the sky. My heart was broken to see such poverty. Poverty there is nothing like what we call it here in the United States. In fact, poor people here are counted among the top 5% of the richest in the world. It did not take long to burn with love for these beautiful, bronze-skinned people and the ministry there.

In fact, the whole time we were there the theme of a marriage union kept arising like sweet incense. The overall sense was that God was joining in a form of marriage, their ministry in India, with which we were partnering and our church from the United States, who sent us. I kept hearing deep in my soul that I should give my ring as a symbol of the union. Finally, overwhelmed by the thought that I had to give the ring to our leaders to seal the union, I called Scott from India and started sharing what was happening. Before I could share the whole story, he said that he thought I should give my engagement ring as a symbol of the union. Well, that was confirmation enough for me. I love how God confirms what He puts deep in our hearts! I quietly shared with one of the leaders, my brother Steve, what was going on and gave him the ring as a symbol, an engagement, for the union. I had only one stipulation, it was not to be shared where it came from. It was to be a gift from our entire team to theirs. We decided to offer it at the ceremony that they had before our departure. Gripped in the sweltering heat of an Indian summer, the hearts of two churches were connected and sealed with the ring that had been now the third engagement promise (Jesus and me, me and Scott, our church and theirs). Funny, until writing this I never realized that there were 3 engagements with the ring, a trinity! How like the Father to continually connect dots so effortlessly!

When we arrived home from India there was much to do for the wedding, including purchasing wedding bands. My dad and I went out to lunch one day and he shared that he would like to give, to Scott and me, his and my mom's wedding bands. My mom had died several years earlier but they had celebrated 45 years of anniversaries before her death! This simple gesture made with simple gold bands meant more than any words I could possibly pen here. This was such a treasured gift. I burst into tears and profusely thanked my dad who had become my best friend. The thought also crossed my mind that perhaps this is why the Lord had me give my white gold ring away. The two would not have worked well together in color or shape. With that, I put the thought of the engagement ring to rest knowing that God had worked it out perfectly, as He always does. We had our wedding a month later, and moved to Ohio, where Scott lived. We started attending his church. This was very new as his church was huge and the one we came from was very small. I mused that it looked like the inside of an airport, coffee bar and all. I so wanted to have a friend there so I did not feel so alone. Wouldn't you know that God already had one waiting for me? My first friend there was a precious lady who worked with children with autism (my new step-daughter Colleen was one of the children she worked with).

This precious friend is instrumental in the story of the rings and in Matt's life story. She is a writer as well and wrote an incredible vacation bible school (VBS) adventure called Outback Adventure for the church we attended. The main character, an Australian treasure hunter, was to be played by a man. Unfortunately she could not find a man available for the whole week of VBS, so she asked Matt. Now, at this point in his life, Matt was extremely timid and shy, but by some miracle of God, he said yes. She lovingly mentored him in acting and presenting a great Australian accent. This connected all of us in a supernatural way. Matt continued on to learn to play the guitar and piano and has become a worship leader, thanks in part to this early encouragement by her.

But that's not why I shared this. Fast-forward until the time just after our prayer for provision for an engagement ring.

We were having a women's conference at my current church. The name of the conference was "Hidden Treasures". We also had a "Women in Business Marketplace" set up for the women to browse, shop, and learn about different organizations. Our organization, Assert Now, Inc. which is a charitable non-profit organization that exists to educate awareness, equip prevention, and empower restoration from victimizations like abuse, human trafficking, and bullying, was encouraged to have a booth. Since I was one of the key leaders for the conference, I was not able to man our table. So my friend, the writer, and now our organizations' executive administrator, agreed to man the table. Matt's girlfriend, Nicke, also helped out. Throughout the conference, the two of them sat together. It was at the end of the conference when this friend, the one who God connected in so many ways so long ago, heard from God that she was supposed to give Matt an engagement ring!!! Seriously…I am not kidding! She knew nothing about them even thinking about getting married, or mine and Matt's secret prayer to the Lord!

She asked if I had a few minutes to chat before she left the conference. Of course I said yes! She proceeded to say that she wanted to make sure it was okay with me (the mom) if she gave Matt an engagement ring to propose to Nicke when he wanted. I was floored! I could not believe it. Tears ran down my cheeks as I said yes and shared with her the story up to this point because…wait for it…there is more!! She could not believe the long connection either. She said she would bring it to the staff meeting the following week.

Okay – so you know there is more to this story. After she told me about the ring and I had a good cry, I shared it with Matt who also broke out in tears. AMAZING that God answered this prayer so quickly. It was a matter of weeks. There are some prayers and actual night-time dreams I have been waiting on for over 30 years, as you will see in later chapters. This was a very quick and pointed answer to a specific prayer! Matt asked me the question that never even occurred to me, "Do you know what it looks like?" I assumed it would be perfect and never even thought to ask her. My answer to him may have seemed canned or rehearsed but it is what came out immediately, "It's from God. I am sure it will be beautiful, perfect!" With that we waited for the following week, excited and a little overwhelmed.

The day we were supposed to get the ring, I met with my best friend Kari, in the morning. You will hear more about Kari later in this book as she has also been instrumental in so much of my journey over the last 10 years. She is an incredible friend, sister in Christ, and adventure buddy! Anyway, I started to share the story of the rings with her. She seemed to be amazed at the part of the story where I gave away my ring so many years ago. I thought it was so cool how what I lovingly sacrificed so long ago, God blessed forward to my son! She asked incredulously, "So you don't have an engagement ring?" I said no and began my girl talk about how I had looked at rings over the years but would just not spend the money for one because there were other priorities. She looked at me and exclaimed, "I have a ring for you!" "What?" I said dumbfounded. She proceeded to tell me her story of the ring she had found many years ago. She had spent considerable time advertising for its owner to be found. When no one claimed the ring, she buried it in her drawer, forgetting it even existed. She said she had not thought about it in years until I was telling her the story and God told her she needed to give it to me. She said to wait a minute while she pulled out the HIDDEN TREASURE" from her drawer. WOW – Hidden Treasures are becoming a theme here! At this point I really could not believe what God was doing. I sat a little dazed and astounded with His presence.

She brought out the ring and proceeded to tell me that it appraised back then at $2500. She continued by saying that I could sell it if I wanted but it was mine to do whatever I wanted. Of course, I will not sell it. I wear it as a proud reminder of just how great our God is! But, wait for it, that's not all. As I got into my van and praised the Lord for his extravagant and lavish outpouring, Matt's question popped in my head, "What does his ring look like?" Instantly, I the Lord said, "It looks like yours."

I have been praying for my daughter-in-laws since my boys were in the womb. Matt's girlfriend was not exactly who I was expecting. In fact, the Lord really purified my heart through this process and burned away deep judgments I did not realize existed in my heart. There is a whole story to share about this but it will have to wait for later! To say the very least, Nicke is perfectly suited for Matt! Just what I had hoped for in a daughter-in-law! God showed me that the ring was sealing her and my hearts together as well. That night as we met and received the engagement ring, I pulled it out of the velvet bag with which it was placed and, WAIT FOR IT...

It looked almost exactly like my ring. It was just a little smaller and the side diamonds were arranged in a different way. From the top of it though it looks like the same ring. Crazy, right!!! So let's process this: 2 rings, many hearts joined in this long journey and one amazing God delivering them the same day. Unbelievable!!!! Step by step each story unfolds. Sometimes it is not until years later that we look back and see with clarity all the connections. If we WAIT FOR IT... our prayers and God's promises manifest, and it is worth it!

I have heard it said that the journey of a thousand miles begins with a single step. A single step in a faith walk may seem small, but as you just heart the little things, sometimes a simple, heartfelt prayer for help, can add up to BIG testimonies over time.

Chapter 2

THE SMALL THINGS

"God does not care about the small things. He has too many BIG things to take care of."

This is probably the **BIGGEST** lie I have ever been told in my life. The saddest part of it is that millions of people walk around each day believing this. Unfortunately, I was one of them for many years. You may even believe it. If you do, stay with me and see if you believe it when we are through. How do I know it is a lie? To me it's simple, if God numbers the hairs on our head, Luke 12:7, *"Indeed, the very hairs of your head are all numbered. Don't be afraid; you are worth more than many sparrows,"* then why would He dismiss any seemingly small thing? It's a matter of perspective!! *Perspective is everything.* I recently heard Bill Johnson of Bethel Church in Redding, California say **"Supernatural intervention gives a change of perspective"**. I love this truth. Now, "supernatural intervention" may sound really big or churchy but it is really simple. It is God moving in our life in a way that is beyond what we can accomplish ourselves or beyond how we typically respond. For example, if someone really hurt your feelings and you just forgave them and forgot it and then thought, wow, I would usually respond differently. That is supernatural intervention changing perspective. It will help to understand this as you read on. I love the expression, **"Each day is a gift, that is why it is called the**

present"! When you face a life or death situation, you realize just how precious each day is! The birds singing sounds sweeter, the green grass looks more vivid, and each moment is more treasured.

I do tend to look at the cup at least half if not all the way full and with what some might call rose colored glasses. This does help my perspective to look towards the positive. It all goes back to perspective. Attitude changes everything. Right now you have probably already formed an opinion or attitude about something I have written. It is okay, we all do. I am just challenging you to look to the positive, or the triumphant, in every situation. There is always a better past the bitter, you just have to wait for it! It may be hard to find at times but prayer will reveal it sooner or later. My perspective at times has been laughed at and deemed crazy or "too spiritualized". Inside I have even believed these opinions and allowed my joy to be robbed. I have also believed that I am a failure, unsuccessful, too young at times, now too old, and seemingly useless. Many of these came from the world around me and other people's perspective. If you have ever felt this way, you know that whether spoken or unspoken, these thoughts hit you right in the soul. These lies of the enemy, Satan, can be overwhelming and paralyzing. The truth and good news is that God is greater than Satan. In fact scripture tells us in Romans 16:19 *"God will crush Satan under our feet"*. The **difficulty comes when we have to take action and play a role in the freedom from defeat**. That's right. **We do play a**

huge part in this life. In fact, you are the star and leading lady or man of your life, don't give the role away for a lesser part. **We can choose our thoughts and our actions.** It takes hard work but it is achievable. We may want God to just ZAP us and make everything work but He is a gentleman, He does not push where we do not want change, even when we need it. <u>**God does not want puppets. He wants partners, intimate and active.**</u> Aligning thoughts with a Heavenly perspective reaps Heavenly riches; IT...IS...A...CHOICE!

Mines in the Mind

I have had to take drastic measures to contain the battle that rages in my mind. The mines that explode, causing me to have painful fragmented shards of worry lodged in my brain, triggering a downward spiral along dangerous paths, has had to be dealt with severely. I needed to change my perspective and attitude. The BEST way I have found to diffuse these mines is to pull out the bad shards or thoughts and replace them with good ones. There are many passages in the Bible that the Lord has given us to wage war in this battle. My favorite one and a life saver for me when my thoughts head in a bad direction is:

2 Corinthians 10:5 (NIV), "We demolish arguments and every pretension that sets itself up against the knowledge of God, and we take captive every thought to make it obedient to Christ."

Literally, when intrusive thoughts come (they are different for everyone) from the enemy, from negative self-talk, wherever, when those mines threaten to explode, I yell in my head, unless I am by myself, then I yell out loud (it's fun) "Take captive my thoughts in obedience to Christ". This process used to happen many times throughout the day until His word drowned out my own spinning, worrisome thoughts, or the enemy's lies, either way, until I was back to my identity in Christ and not the lie that was trying to take root! Fortunately, the intrusive thoughts are less and less. If you think, this isn't me, I don't need this tool, let me give you some examples of ways you may be hurting yourself: How about the thoughts that say, "You are fat, ugly, worthless, stupid, a screw up" or on the other hand, the thoughts that say to someone else, "You are a moron, why don't you just shut up, you idiot, you are stupid, you don't know what you are talking about", I'm sure you can relate. **What we embrace in our mind, we declare as truth in our life**. The next time you think, "I am a failure, useless, a rotten parent, the world would be better off without me, no one likes me", and it goes on and on, **SHOUT WITH ME "TAKE CAPTIVE MY THOUGHTS"**, do it until you cannot even remember the damaging thoughts you were thinking. Then replace them with truth! ***I placed a list of scriptural declarations at the back of the book!***

It works, trust me, I have had to do it even writing these pages as the enemy raged "No one cares what you have to say"! Well, I am taking captive those thoughts! I am going to finish this with God as my witness and partner as I continue on!

Chapter 3

IDENTITY

In the last 12 years the Lord has really challenged me to grow exponentially and embrace my identity in Him! Of course it has been forming my whole life but these years have been intentionally focused on walking in the power and love that I have through Jesus. I have had some amazing refiners over the past few years! It is never just one way that God touches me/us. The more that I live the more I realized that this amazing journey spans generations and multitudes of people! Our identity, our very eternal heritage reaches back to the Garden of Eden. **Part of our heritage is to have dominion over the earth and all living things as given by God in Genesis**. WOW – to really think about that is mind blowing yet simple at the same time!

Genesis 1:26 - Then God said, "Let us make mankind in our image, in our likeness, so that they may rule over the fish in the sea and the birds in the sky, over the livestock and all the wild animals, and over all the creatures that move along the ground."

Then Jesus shares the power we have through His resurrection and sending the Holy Spirit to us by stating,

John 14:12, 26 (NIV) "14 Very truly I tell you, whoever believes in me will do the works I have been doing, and they will do even greater things than these, because I am going to the Father".

"26 But the Advocate, the Holy Spirit, whom the Father will send in my name, will teach you all things and will remind you of everything I have said to you."

Now that's dominion and authority! This truth is where this book's inspirational faith journey begins, or for me, continues. I have experienced some of the **GREATER** things and it is awesome to be a part of that connection and power. Jesus healed the sick, raised the dead, open the eyes of the blind, and caste out demons. If you take a chance and read the New Testament of the Bible, you will find example after example of these things. I can attest to doing some of these same things with the Holy Spirit as my partner. Yes, I have been a part of praying and having someone medically dead be raised to life. I recently had dinner with this man and his wife and he reminded me that after he was resurrected he was then pronounced blind and disabled. We had a good laugh and praise God moment. God not only raised him from the dead but restored his health and sight as well.

I have been a part of deaf people hearing, legs growing, peace returning, hives disappearing, demons fleeing, trauma victims being restored; all through the power of love and the Holy Spirit with which God gave **US**, **ME**, when Jesus went to be seated at the right hand of God the Father. In Acts 1:8 (NIV), it is shared:

"But you will receive power when the Holy Spirit comes on you; and you will be my witnesses in Jerusalem, and in all Judea and Samaria, and to the ends of the earth."

This all happened when Jesus was crucified and raised from the dead to ascend into Heaven.

You do not have to look far or hard in the Bible to find the rich inheritance we have in Christ Jesus. I stand firm that **truth is truth whether you want to believe it or not**. There has been a great deal of historical evidence that Christ's life and the accounts of miracles are true as well. My own life is a testament to the truth and treasures in the Bible. My life was powerless when I did not embrace my inheritance and identity in Christ. Now it is full of love and power to share with all, **yes even those who are hiding, pretending not to be lost as I was for so long**! Remember my old self-talk it has been transformed by the renewing of my mind and now sounds like this, "I am a princess, daughter of the Most High King Jesus. I was bought at a heavy price of love and sacrifice by God who came to earth to be tortured and killed, only to rise again so that I may be forgiven and free! Through the glorious richness that I have so freely received, not by any work of my own but through Jesus' AMAZING love, I am set free to set the captives free!" Amen, just saying it again gives me a fresh indwelling of His glory!! Proclaim this out loud and embrace the power. Oh and if you are a male you can replace princess with prince. This is our RICH inheritance …our **IDENTITY**.

Ongoing Journey

When the Lord finally got through to me fully, I was a single mom and started running after Him wholeheartedly as a Bride to Christ. I remember sitting in a sermon at a church in Centerville, OH. One part of the sermon was particularly powerful for me. It was a simple truth shared, "Jesus was a friend to prostitutes and tax collectors". For me, the story of the Samaritan Woman was all too real. I felt such shame from my past relationships, addictions, and failures. This simple truth hit me hard and heavy. Tears spilled from me. It was the first time I truly understood the power of Jesus' love for me.

No matter what I had done or what shame and condemnation I carried from what had been done to me, or even how close I danced to the edge of disaster and disobedience, **<u>JESUS LOVED ME, HE JUST SIMPLY LOVED ME!</u>** He was waiting for me to turn back to Him so that He could give me all that He had for me. It seemed like in an instant the weight of this truth came crashing down. I suddenly could relate to myself as the child in the "Parable of the Lost Son" in Luke 15:11-32(NIV). One reason I feel it was written was to show God's love to me and anyone else who had chosen this wayward path and wanted to come home. If you have not read it or even if you have, read it below. Try to gain a new perspective from it!! It is powerful!

Jesus continued:

"11 There was a man who had two sons. 12 The younger one said to his father, 'Father, give me my share of the estate.' So he divided his property between them. 13 "Not long after that, the younger son

got together all he had, set off for a distant country and there squandered his wealth in wild living. *14* After he had spent everything, there was a severe famine in that whole country, and he began to be in need. *15* So he went and hired himself out to a citizen of that country, who sent him to his fields to feed pigs. *16* He longed to fill his stomach with the pods that the pigs were eating, but no one gave him anything. *17* "When he came to his senses, he said, 'How many of my father's hired servants have food to spare, and here I am starving to death! *18* I will set out and go back to my father and say to him: Father, I have sinned against heaven and against you. *19* I am no longer worthy to be called your son; make me like one of your hired servants.' *20* So he got up and went to his father. "But while he was still a long way off, his father saw him and was filled with compassion for him; he ran to his son, threw his arms around him and kissed him. *21* "The son said to him, 'Father, I have sinned against heaven and against you. I am no longer worthy to be called your son.' *22* "But the father said to his servants, 'Quick! Bring the best robe and put it on him. Put a ring on his finger and sandals on his feet. *23* Bring the fattened calf and kill it. Let's have a feast and celebrate. *24* For this son of mine was dead and is alive again; he was lost and is found.' So they began to celebrate. *25* "Meanwhile, the older son was in the field. When he came near the house, he heard music and dancing. *26* So he called one of the servants and asked him what was going on. *27* 'Your brother has come,' he replied, 'and your father has killed the fattened calf because he has him back safe and sound.' *28* "The older brother became angry and refused to go in. So his father went out and pleaded with him. *29* But he answered his father, 'Look! All these years I've been slaving for you and never disobeyed your orders.

Yet you never gave me even a young goat so I could celebrate with my friends. 30 But when this son of yours who has squandered your property with prostitutes comes home, you kill the fattened calf for him!' 31 "'My son,' the father said, 'you are always with me, and everything I have is yours. 32 But we had to celebrate and be glad, because this brother of yours was dead and is alive again; he was lost and is found.'"

This is what we do when we willfully run away from God's best for our life and into a destructive path, wallowing with the pigs and spending years of our money and precious time running after mediocrity and mayhem. Thank goodness God's word promises us in Romans 8:28,

"And we know that in all things God works for the good of those who love him, who[a] have been called according to his purpose."

Even when we turn our back on God, He redeems us when we turn back! I did not truly live until I finally believed that **God was not angry, vindictive, or unhappy with me!** He simply loves me and wants the best for me! We cannot embrace this fully if we are walking in sin because we operate conditionally, whereas walking righteously in Kingdom principles operates unconditionally.

It was in the spring of the following year, after having the radical truth that I was loved unconditionally by Jesus, that I attended my first Women of Faith conference in the Midwest. At this point in my life I was a single mom just trying to raise my boys and cling to Jesus without any distractions. Some amazing ladies from my church sponsored me to go to the event with them. I was completely overwhelmed by the power and presence of the Holy Spirit in the place. I could barely sing or stand being overcome with tears of joy! There must have been 20,000 women praising the Lord and enjoying the speakers.

During worship the Holy Spirit whispered to me, "You will be one of these speakers someday". "YEAH, RIGHT", I shouted in my head!! I remember being horrified at the thought of getting up before even 2 women, much less 20,000 women, to be subjected to judgment and ridicule. Unfortunately, that is what I have experienced with many women including myself. We judge clothes, make-up, hair, weight, motives, and anything else, to make ourselves feel better? Does it work? Absolutely not! It only promotes bitterness, anger, rage, and envy. Since I have chosen to live unoffended without judgment towards others I have found freedom from worrying what others thought, but it was a battle! Anyway, the whisper broke in to my spinning thoughts and grew louder until it began to turn into a full blown, as if it were happening in the physical, encounter with the living God.

Suddenly I was on the stage. I felt confused for a minute and blinked to adjust my eyes to the brightness of the lights. There were several sensations and feelings encompassing me. I could feel God bumps (some people call them goose bumps) all over me and I felt as if I would burst from fear and excitement. As my eyes began to focus, I could see a multitude of faces staring back at me, expectantly. There was a silence in the room and I could hear my anxious breathing. I could sense the power of the Holy Spirit. Jesus was standing next to me and it felt like I was on fire. I could feel a push in my spirit to speak to the masses staring and sensed that if I denied the urge to speak I would spontaneously combust. That whisper, such a still small and quiet voice had now manifested in an all-out full-blown God encounter.

I do not know how long it lasted. I could not tell you anything else that happened during it. All I remember is that when worship ended, it had passed but the powerful presence and impact of the encounter has lasted. As the conference continued, I had completely dismissed it as the enemy trying to make me think I was something special. OH MY GOSH, even as I am typing this **I cringe at how warped my/our thoughts can be at times and the way we can stomp on our own destiny!** WOW, I am so glad that the Lord is patient with me when I argue with Him and dismiss encounters.

When I came back from the event, the precious lady that had watched my young sons greeted me at the door. Before she moved to let me pass, she drew in a sharp breath and exclaimed almost shouting at me, "You had an encounter with God. You are glowing! You are radiating! What did He say? What is He showing you for your life?" **I was truly BLOWN AWAY!** Wait a minute, I thought, if I was just trying to exalt myself, how did she see this? How could she know? How could she travel into the deepest part of my being and sense what had just happened? Was it that evident? I wondered if she could see my sheer terror about what I had been told.

I revisited the brief but powerful encounter with her. She exclaimed, "Then it will be so"! With that she invited me in and we casually chatted about the boys for a few minutes and then I left. I have not spoken to her since that time. I honestly cannot even remember her name but I have never forgotten her declaration. I have continued to WAIT FOR IT ever since, walking in step with the Holy Spirit. There was a season I ran from this encounter, refusing to believe that I would have the courage to do what the Lord had shown me. How could I speak before anyone when I shook violently inside when I walked into a room of strangers by myself? My dialog with the Lord was "I need a lot of work for that to happen"! God's response, "With me all things are possible"! After a few years of running, I started to grow rapidly in my confidence and began speaking with women's groups and mom's groups and teaching martial arts, self-defense and trainings through Assert.

Chapter 4

SPIRITUAL GIFTS

Walking in faith in this new season of my life, with a "death" diagnosis hanging in the air, has given me an even stronger resolve to live radically for Jesus, embracing with joy everything put before me, whether trial or triumph because in the end, it's all triumph! I think it is important to understand the journey that has enabled me to WAIT FOR IT, the promise to be fulfilled, while walking in faith.

The encounter amidst the great women of faith in that auditorium with Jesus at my side still remains in the depths of my spirit. One of the main things I learned over those years was how to more effectively use my spiritual gifts and what their purpose is from the Bible. 1 Corinthians 12, 13, 14 are great chapters to read about these gifts. I had known since I was a little girl that I could sense good and evil. I could see angels and demons, for me though they did not appear as you see dramatized on television and the movies. Maybe some people see into the spiritual realm that way, but I do not. It is more subtle, like flashes of them. Silhouetted light and dark shapes, energy figures, is the best way I can describe the encounters. I also knew that I would sense things before they happened and many times could see into the future. Of course **the enemy seeks to counterfeit these gifts by labeling them as psychic abilities and diminishing**

them to our own inner strength and cosmic happenings.

It did not take me long in my early twenties to learn that the things I could sense and see were better left inside of me than sharing them. There were countless times I offended someone or scared them to the point that they just did not want to talk to me anymore. The scary part for me was that these things that I saw, heard, sensed, or felt were more right than wrong. Events I saw in my mind or dreams eventually came to pass. These two things I discovered were a gift of discernment and a prophetic gift.

It is dangerous to walk around with these gifts and not understand them! Both for you and the person you vomit all over with your words. That is a whole other book I am working on "Wearing Your Gifts Well". It is one of my favorite areas to teach on, walking clothed in love, peace, and the understanding of your spiritual gifts! I also love seeing them manifest in children's lives. It is so important for parents to walk with their children and help mentor them to grow powerfully and wholly in their love relationship with Jesus Christ and understand how to operate with the Holy Spirit. Spiritual gifts are not for our personal benefit but for the benefit of the body of Christ.

I also spent a lot of time studying spiritual warfare because I knew that I was in the middle of a war between the forces of darkness and light. Ephesians 6:10-20 tells us that our battle is not against flesh and blood but of spiritual forces. I battled every day with some kind of dark difficulty in those years before 2003. One book that really made an impact on me, Worship Warrior, discussed how spiritual ascension is important for us to be full of God's glory to release healing and love on the earth. In the book, Chuck D. Pierce states, "Once we go up to the Throne Room and gain revelation from the Father, we descend (spiritual not physical) and begin to share it down here on earth" (p. 76). The front of the book states "ascending in worship, descending in war". This does not mean to imply physical aggression but a spiritual state of connectedness with our Divine Creator to combat the spiritual darkness in our lives and others!

SHAZAM, there it was, the key that unlocked so many doors for me! When I was connected to the Lord, I had no problem understanding what and how to use my gifts! I have learned how important it is to keep the connection, **take the time to abide with Jesus, be full of the presence so that it may radiate from me without even uttering a word**. It has been a life-time learning process, one in which I am sure I will continue until the day I see Jesus face to face in Heaven or here on earth!

I also studied strategic warfare. I loved learning about the hierarchy of angels and demons so that I better understood how to combat the enemy. For me it is simple, the enemy does not get glory from me. I set my mind on things above…. In fact, one day I had severe stomach pains. They were so bad I thought I was going to pass out. I was sitting praying like mad, "pain leave in Jesus' name", over and over again. I finally heard Jesus say, "What are you doing?" I replied, "PRAYING", and "What are you focusing your prayer on" asked Jesus? WOW it hit me like a ton of bricks! I was focusing on the pain instead of the healer. Instantly I began singing my favorite love song to Jesus. My son Matt wrote it! It changes the atmosphere from fear to love every time! Such a simple truth but so easily overlooked. We look at circumstance instead of the one who overcame the most difficult circumstance.

LOVE IS THE GREATEST DEFEATER OF FEAR AND DARKNESS!

1 John 4:18 (ESV) "There is no fear in love, but perfect love casts out fear. For fear has to do with punishment, and whoever fears has not been perfected in love".

I think fear is one of the greatest evils and most destructive forces I have seen. We see it in our current global realm as war and terrorism heightens. For me, this scripture elevates the level of understanding in how to combat evil...**LOVE**! So many times I have found if I am willing to put my fear, pride, control, envy, angry, bitterness, anxiety, and frustration aside, the enemy has lost any foothold he may have temporarily gained. If I am abiding in Christ, and spending time with the Father as Christ did, I am full of the spiritual weapon I need to win these battles! **LOVE!!**

The more I pressed into God's word and the wisdom filled teachings of my fellow brothers and sisters in Christ, the more I grew to understand who I am and what I was being called to do with the Lord. It should have been simple; having been shown to me over and over again by visions the Lord gave me! Life, busyness, and discouragement blotted out the purpose God had planned for me. I have had so many visions. I am sure you have too. I will share this one in particular as it has become the overarching goal and passion for my life's journey with Christ.

Chapter 5

A VISION FOR THE FUTURE

It was in the fall of 2011. My friend Kari asked me if I wanted to go to a prophecy conference at The International House of Prayer (IHOP) in Kansas City, MO. She said she wanted to pay for the trip if I wanted to go! I was just minding my business in my seemingly ordinary life when this extraordinary thing happened. How many times does someone offer to pay all expenses for you to go away to a place you have been longing to go for years?

My first response was, **"ABSOLUTELY!"** Of course, I had my husband and children, then 13 and 17, to think about. I had prayed so long to go to IHOP, I figured this was Papa God's answer. My family was fine with it. Both Kari and I were very excited and sensed that this was going to be a **POWERFUL** journey.

We headed out on Wednesday morning, excited and anticipating what the Lord was going to do over the next few days. We arrived; surprised to find that IHOP was not a fancy "mega-church" but a very modest and humble yet large building that resembled a warehouse. Still "mega" in numbers, it brought a refreshing spin on my church building perspective. There were several things that happened during our stay including a vision/encounter I had with Jesus for my future.

During one of the very powerful worship sets, I heard a song that I had never heard before called "Holy". I had never felt the power of the Lord fall as heavily as I did when they started this song. It seemed like a heavy blanket covered the room. I felt a bit dizzy yet extremely clear in my thoughts. It sounded like I was in the midst of the multitude of Heavenly hosts singing "Holy, Holy, Holy is the Lord God Almighty". I sensed the Lord trying to break through and show me something. I started to tremble and could hardly stand. I was spell-bound, frozen, and not able to sing, move, or for that matter, breathe. I could feel tears pouring down my face like a gentle waterfall. Suddenly, before me Jesus appeared. It was as if the rest of the world disappeared and just He and I were standing face to face.

I remember feeling His Presence was like an all-consuming fire, searing with a heat that was unimaginable, intense, like standing in the middle of a huge bon fire, yet I was not burned or unable to stand in it. His hair was brown but glowed like finely polished gold. His eyes were fiery brown, flashing like flames from the fire, yet gentle and loving at the same time. As I stood in front of Him, unable to move or take my eyes off of Him, I remember thinking that I should not be able to gaze into His eyes. He is the Savior of the universe. I should drop dead from looking at Him. Yet I remained, eyes locked and spell-bound staring into the fiery pools. Next, He did something very surprising; actually

unbelievable, if I had not been a part of the encounter I probably would have been horrified to see it. He reached into His chest and scooped out His heart. It was not bloody or gross but a quick and simple act. It looked like a human heart you might see on one of the medical channels broadcasting a heart transplant. He then tenderly and lovingly placed it in my hands. They shook from the pulsing of his heart. The warmth of this loving act consumed me with a deep burning fire inside. I remember feeling the heaviness of the weight of His heart in my hands. It beat rhythmically, systematically in perfect sync with my own heart. This was unfathomable!!! Jesus' heart was in my hands. Mind blowing numbness now consumed me. What would happen next? How could I be entrusted with such a priceless gift? Was it a gift or was He trying to show me how heavy His heart was for those He loved? So many questions and thoughts raced through my mind.

Swiftly, but gently, as if reading my thoughts and seeking to still them with the answer, Jesus placed His hands beneath my hands, that were still trembling from holding His heart. His hands were rugged yet soft like velvet. The color of His skin was golden bronze. There were no pierce marks from the cross because He stood in His resurrected form. I felt slight pressure on my hands as he lightly and affectionately lifted His heart to my chest. He pressed our hands against my chest and instantly, His heart was transplanted into my chest. Once inside of me, I could feel the beating of my heart quicken and the sound amplify as if someone was beating out the timing on a drum as well. Then He told me that His heart was now my heart for His people. I would love them unconditionally and see them as He sees them. He again impressed upon me that I was now HIS HEART. Just as quickly as He had appeared and this happened, He was gone and I could move again! I was stunned. I wanted to cry out for Him to come back but He was already gone. I did not know what to do so I sat down and sobbed as "Holy" continued to ring out through the room. I remember thinking that every color I saw was more vibrant than I had ever seen. His robe was a rich purple, his eyes were blazing with every color I had ever seen in fire and then some that I had not seen before. His heart was the most beautiful scarlet red. His hands were a golden bronze as if he was glowing.

UNBELIEVEABLE!

I have always had a heart for and felt connected to people - all people, but particularly those who seemed downcast or poor in spirit; people who have been beaten down by life's discouragements and those who have been victimized and left in their pain and bitterness. Even before I had any of my "formal" training in counseling and inner healing, I would encourage those God highlighted or drew me to. I found myself many times in my teen and early adult years, walking up to total strangers saying that I sensed God wanted me to hug them, encourage them, tell them He loved them, ask them if they needed help. Whatever I positively sensed, I would share. The things I saw that were negative, I would not mention because I had learned the pain of sharing them and the isolation from them hitting their unwelcomed mark.

When I do this now, I ask the Lord for more insight, so that I can pray for the person that I had the word of knowledge about and share it in a wisdom-filled and positive, encouraging way. This is what prophetic words are for, as stated in 1 Corinthians 14:3, "But the one who prophesies speaks to people for their strengthening, encouraging and comfort." I have had lots of training now in what spiritual gifts are and how they are used. I also know that we are called to love. This vision was taking me to a whole new awareness of this! For me, it was not a call to love and go into the world; it was a transformation in me to be love, His love. Even now, it is hard to explain, I just know that it is who I am in Him.

Two years later I went with one of the leaders on my team at church to visit some precious friends at a house of prayer/ministry in Stryker, OH. One of their leaders was going to do a private training for us on silk banner painting. She is an incredible dancer and artist, not to mention a very strong woman of faith and sister in Christ. I knew that this time would be special and, of course, POWERFUL because the Lord is with us.

One of the things that she had us do in preparation of for our painting was to spend a good deal of time in the prayer room asking Jesus what vision He had for our life. She believed that in order to truly embrace the experience of making a life banner, you should have a vision from God. Whatever He gave us in this vision was what we were going to paint on the silk banner.

We proceeded to spend hours in the prayer room. I loved this prayer room. I have met Jesus here several times. When I was there, it was set up like a beautiful garden. In my mind, He and I would walk hand in hand through it. I thought of those times with Him and so many other things the Lord had showed me in that room. My mind seemed to drift from encounter to encounter. After a while, I began to experience the encounter at IHOP. I started thinking that I was just remembering it because it was so powerful and COOL, so I tried to make it go away.

The harder I tried, the more it manifested in front of me, I sensed the Lord gently admonish me and say for me to humble myself and let Him finish the vision. I was both taken aback and excited! I thought the vision was complete and I had been trying to love those around and walk unoffended like Jesus even more since the first encounter. I immediately asked for forgiveness for my haughtiness and relaxed back into the silky, comfy pillows and waited for more.

I again began to see the Lord standing in front of me with His heart pounding, rhythmically in His hands. This time, His head was like the sun, shooting colorful rainbow rays in all directions, too powerful to look directly at. His robe was the same richest, most vibrant purple I had ever seen. He placed His heart once again in my hands and then placed it in my chest. As I continued to watch, the most extraordinary thing happened. Within my chest the heart split open and a stunning, blinding, light shot out from my heart. There wasn't just one stream of light but rays that hit everything I could see and far off to where I couldn't see. Suddenly, stretched out before me I could see what looked like millions of people standing in the distance. There was a sea of heads, all colors and cultures, with which the light was falling. They all seemed connected to one another. His message seared through my body, I was being called to be a light to the nations and multitudes for Jesus! I was being commissioned to travel throughout the world to touch people for the Lord. I sensed this was not just a call given to all believers to "go and make disciples of all nations" (Matthew 28:18). It was a radical faith walk into the unknown with the Holy Spirit as my guide. This meant to love them as He loved them with unconditional love, mercy, and grace! To set an example of what **REAL LOVE** and truth looked like. I then saw a rainbow above us. It was flashing with lightning and brilliant colors! He said it was the sign of His promise to fulfill this vision. When the vision had ended, I realized that my shirt was wet with tears. I had no idea how long I was sitting there weeping but I knew for sure that I had encountered Jesus again. I also knew that I had to start pursuing this vision more wholeheartedly. I needed to forgive more, give more mercy and grace, and ultimately **LOVE more!!!** There was no time or place for bitterness, pride, or anything else that was not from the Holy Spirit! The more I aligned myself with righteousness, the more I found an open Heaven over me and all that I touched.

After we had both received our visions, we painted the silk banners, which turned out to be beautiful expressions of the visions He had given each of us. I have named it the "I AM LOVE" banner!

Reflecting back on this, my life has been a tapestry colored over and over again with this message of shining His light to the world. My very name means dawn or the synonyms: dawning, day, daybreak, daylight, light, morn, morning, sun, sunrise, sun up. In my early adolescent years I hated my name because kids found a way to twist it and make it seem terrible. They laughed at me and mocked me with unkind names that rhymed with my name. I am sure you get the picture so I do not have to put any extra thoughts into your head. With anger and bitterness in my heart as a deflated teen, I asked my mom why she would give me a name that caused me such grief. She sat me down and soothed my dejected spirit with the following explanation. She shared that she named me after the Roman goddess of the Dawn, Aurora. She said that the Lord had given her the name before I was even born. She had looked it up to find out what it meant and found the information on the dawn. She then said that she knew that I would be a GREAT LIGHT for God someday. Since the name Aurora meant light, she thought it was perfect. I have since mused and found it funny that she named me after a god that she did not believe in to be a light for the God that she did believe in. Nevertheless, I have come to realize that this destiny of my life was given before God placed me in my mother's womb. Jeremiah 1:5a (NIV) states,

"Before I formed you in the womb I knew[a] you, before you were born I set you apart".

I truly believe that each of us has a unique mission here on earth, one that we were created to complete if we so choose. If I am correct, and I believe that it is scriptural truth, you may be sitting on a destiny that wants to unfold itself. Perhaps you have not considered this before. If you find that hard to believe or accept, start searching through the Bible, contact me, your pastor, any of the teachers I have shared in the book. There are answers to your treasure map just waiting to be discovered.

I do believe that my name describes me well. I enjoy spreading joy and light! I have no greater satisfaction than sharing love with others whether through a kind word, deed, a "holy hug" or just spending time with them. In fact, when my season in this life passes, my prayer is that I will be remembered as someone who loved God with everything in me and out of the overflow of His love, I was able to passionately love everyone who crossed my path. I want His beautiful radiant glory to leak from my very pores!

I have actively been seeking ways to learn to be a carrier of God's presence and share His love more tangibly since I painted my silk banner.

Chapter 6

THE MOUNTAIN TOP

On August 27, 2013, after prayerful consideration, I wrote the check to take the Dayton School of Supernatural Ministry Class (DSSM is modeled after the teachings of the Bethel School of Supernatural Ministry in Redding, CA). I had been praying to be able to go to Bethel's school for quite a while, years. I was extremely thrilled that the Lord brought a version of it to me!! I mailed in my check with the hope of taking my life journey with Christ to a new level. What was even more delightful was that my oldest son, Matt, wanted to take the class too!

I share about this leap of faith to take the class because every time I seek to grow more in my walk with Jesus, there is always a new challenge. I love to see just how GREAT OUR GOD is while navigating through challenges. 1 John 4:4 (NIV) says,

"You, dear children, are from God and have overcome them, because the one who is in you is greater than the one who is in the world."

I love this promise of being an overcomer in the Kingdom. Little did I know, at the time, that a HUGE health challenge would face me and my family in the months ahead? In fact, it is the reason I began to write this book with the Lord, to declare His goodness in the midst of the storm, to encourage everyone to WAIT FOR IT, His promises to be fulfilled. I have lived my life seeking the triumph in every seemingly tragic event. This new challenge was no different. It certainly was going to require me to walk in a renewed faith.

Before I go on about this present health faith journey, I want to share with you what has become lovingly known as our "mountain top" experience. A few summers back, my younger brother Steve decided that we should take a first-ever family vacation with our spouses, kids, and my dad. He started organizing it and even paid for it so we were set to go! There ended up being 22 of us staying in this huge house nestled in the mountains of West Virginia. Everyone who came loves Jesus so we had some great times of family worship, sitting around the fireplace with either of my sons playing the guitar, singing, and ushering in a stronger presence of the Holy Spirit. We also had some awesome prayer time. We even had a mini sermon on Revelation by my brother Dan. It really does not get much better than this, when your biological family is also a part of the body of Christ! I am convinced it was a small sample of heaven on earth.

Anyway, at the top of the mountain was a ski lift which takes you down to a lake. Since it was summer, there were paddle boats and kayaks available to use at the lake free of charge! We spent one glorious day on the lake getting sunburned, paddling and peddling our arms and legs off and getting to share kindness and love to the girls who worked for the resort. I actually forgot about this until I started writing this chapter. The workers were grumpy and quite frustrated when our 20+ person team converged on them. I may have been the same way if I was short-handed and this over-zealous mob came at me all at once. We could tell they were short-handed so we took it upon ourselves to help. Of course we had good intentions but my mom would say that the road to hell was paved with good intentions, which is what I think the workers were feeling. This was not a good choice as they abruptly explained that they were responsible for each life on the beach and water so they had to individually check each watercraft and insure that each life jacket was properly secured. They instructed us to be patient and they would get to us. We felt so bad that we had overstepped our boundaries as we only sought to help. It was definitely a lesson in humility and a reminder to be patient.

I do not always handle other's grumpiness well. I was taken aback by their curtness. In response, I was not as kind as I normally am with those that are obviously under duress. I went back to our chairs and started praying silently in my head (or what some call praying in the spirit). It did not take long for the Lord to show me my poor attitude. Here it is again, attitude and perspective. I knew I had to go apologize. I waited until they had gotten the entire crowd taken care of; more people had arrived which added to the already over populated beach. I finally went up to the one girl who was left on the beach and the one that I had been short with and apologized. I also took the time to thank her for caring so much about each life. You could visibly see her relax. She smiled and told me that no one had ever apologized to her for being rude. I had not thought I had been rude but was not going to allow semantics to ruin a God moment. She thanked me over and over again.

She also explained that they were extremely short-handed and she had been working really long hours. Her partner in work for the day was in the same situation. This moment turned the whole day around. It seemed to me that the beauty around us became even more vibrant and I was reminded that each moment of life has a purpose if we take the time to see what that purpose is and wait for it. During this single moment in time, I realized that for these two young women, I was God's source of kindness, love, and a mighty prayer warrior! I may have been the only "Jesus" they saw all summer. I needed to represent well! We continued to enjoy our day, mindful to take time to chat with the girls when they did not have customers. We also made sure they had water and snacks!

After spending hours on the water and beach I began to feel restless. I asked Scott if we could go back up to the top of the mountain and explore. My niece Megan decided to go with us, so we took the ski lift back up to the top to see what kind of stores and things were up there. We walked around for a while and decided to go into a restaurant for a soft drink. Once we were seated, we discovered that they had sweet potato fries, yuuummmmy, one of my favorite things. I did not realize that Megan and I shared this same affinity for sweet potato fries. We ordered them and waited with anticipation for our treat. We were so excited because, as we ate them, we both exclaimed together that we believed that they were probably the best sweet potato fries we had ever tasted! They were the perfect blend of cinnamon, crunch, and sweet! We enjoyed eating and chatting with each other and our waitress. We sat there for over an hour enjoying the peace, air conditioning, and yumminess! We finally paid our bill and got up to leave.

As I got up to leave, I realized that my left knee was killing me. Pain was shooting through it as if someone was slashing it with a knife and at the same time it ached like a migraine headache. Not even thinking anymore about it, I just shrugged it off as sitting too long in an impossibly uncomfortable position. I mentioned it to both Scott and Megan as I limped outside. We said a quick prayer for healing and were off to take the lift back down to the lake. The pain left by the time we boarded the lift and I quickly forgot that it was ever present.

Fast-forward to the next day, everyone wanted to go back to the lake. Unfortunately it was pouring down rain. We all settled into games, books, and conversations realizing that yesterday was a special gift and today would hold its own extraordinary distinction. In the early afternoon, Matt reminded me that I had said I would go get coffee with him at the top of the mountain where the ski lift and restaurants were located. I grumbled because I did not feel like going outside in the pouring rain and now colder temperature. I definitely did not feel like walking the 4 block trek uphill from the parking lot in the tsunami deluge just to get a coffee!

I tried to reason with him but, as only my sons can do, he out-talked me and before I knew it I was getting ready to make the insane journey for a cup of coffee. I was dragging my feet hoping he would change his mind. No such luck, in fact, the opposite happened, he began to hurry me, reminding me that the coffee shop closed early. I found his hastened demeanor quite hilarious. You would understand just how terribly funny this was if you knew Matt. He does not typically move fast for anything. I mean ANYTHING. He marches to a beat of a way different drummer than anyone I know. Most of the time it is a beautiful thing to behold in him as he truly places his trust and life in God's hands which means he does not worry about what the world may think of his timing. Because of this, I found his prompting very interesting to the point of excited anticipation for the journey. It was at that moment that I started to wonder if God had a greater purpose in this adventure than just a cup of coffee! Megan (who was with me yesterday) and Leah, my other niece, wanted to go with us on the caffeine capture mission. Megan also wanted to get some more sweet potato fries even though we had not planned on going to the restaurant. I agreed that we could do that since it would make the drive seem more worthwhile. We all bundled up, loaded up, and headed for the mountain top.

We literally had to run to make it to the coffee shop in time to squeak in 3 minutes before closing! They graciously welcomed us and Matt got his prize, a steaming Venti White Mocha. We retraced our steps back to the restaurant where the scrumptious sweet potato fries were waiting to satisfy our mouth-watering hunger. By now it had stopped raining, leaving the air thick with humidity. The sky still held an ominous look, casting shadows from the clouds, giving the feeling of a prospective torrential downpour. We bounced into the restaurant happy to place the order for our delectable fries!

We were stopped in our tracks by the hostess announcing that Matt could not bring in his coffee, concluding by sharing that it was restaurant policy. His coffee was way too hot for him to finish quickly and too priceless a prize, considering the cost we had just paid in rushing, running, and stress, to throw it away, so we ordered the fries to carry out and sat in the small waiting area outside the restaurant chatting and enjoying the moment of rest from rushing. The same waitress that had served and chatted with us yesterday was there. She smiled confirming recognition and took our order. When the fries were ready, she alerted us. I paid for them and walked out to meet my group. As we left I commented that my left knee was killing me and I could barely walk.

Megan quickly said, "Aunt Aurora it hurt yesterday

too. Maybe someone has a hurt knee and you are feeling their pain like you told me you do sometimes." I had not even considered it until she spoke. We continued to walk to the van discussing, or I should say debating, whether we should go back and ask to pray for someone or not. In the meantime the pain was getting worse. I was feeling pretty strongly that we should go back and so was Megan. Matt and Leah were not so sure. By this time, I knew that we had questioned enough that fear and doubt was beginning to take over. The enemy was winning. In the course of debating our action, we somehow ended up in the van and were driving halfway down the mountain. I could not take it anymore and urged Matt to turn around, as he was driving. Matt found the safest place (although his version includes the testimony that he was the one that wanted to go back, that there were no safe places to turn around, and that we were in mortal danger) and turned the van around. We decided to take the risk!

We retraced our steps and went into the restaurant. I was relieved to see our now familiar waitress was still on duty. She came up and asked if I had forgotten something. I started to stumble with my words and then regained my control and confidence in Jesus. I used to struggle terribly with how to tell someone that I have discerned or felt something, without sounding like a freak and having them laugh at me or tell me I was crazy. Now, even if I stumble, I just share whatever God shows me or I physically feel, with love and sincerity, realizing that if

God leads me to it, He will see me through it! He is my Creator and Judge, no one else should be given that place.

I launched into my usual (for this type of situation anyway), "I hope you do not think this is crazy, but..." I told her that I was a member of a healing prayer team and that I had a sense that someone in the restaurant was having a great deal of pain in their knee and we wanted to pray for them to be healed. I was thankful that she did not look at me like I had two heads. She said, "Hang on and I will ask everyone." I was really surprised at her willingness to jump into this adventure. I was also really glad that she did not make a loud, all-encompassing announcement to draw attention to us! I turned to my entourage and we said a quick "thank you God" that this was looking easier than we thought. Fortunately the restaurant was not packed as my fear manifested into reality and it was now drawing attention and everyone was looking at us.

She came back and said that no one had a pain in their knee. She had asked the few patrons in the restaurant, all of the kitchen help, waiters, and waitresses. I lifted up a prayer in my spirit for Jesus to help us out. Instantaneously my prayer was answered and she said, "Hey, I did not ask the bartender, she may know of someone." Whew, that bought me another few seconds to WAIT FOR IT and figure out how I was going to explain to my young nieces that this is not 100% foolproof.

I sensed I should walk over to the bar with her. The bartender was very nice but said she did not know of anyone who was suffering with knee pain. By now, I was feeling like I could barely walk from the pain. I pleaded with her, "Are you sure you haven't heard of someone in the area with knee pain, even if they are not here right now?" She turned around to look at the almost empty bar. There was one young woman sipping on a soda or pop depending on what part of the world you are from, so the bartender asked her. She explained what was going on and asked if she knew of anyone that matched that description. It felt like hours passed before she said, "Oh my gosh, I do know someone with left knee pain. My good friend injured his knee some time ago on the ski slopes and he is afraid he will not be able to instruct in the coming season. He is a ski instructor for the resort"!

And there it was!!! I almost knocked her over with a hug! I was so excited and greatly relieved! My Jesus came through in the 11th hour when I was truthfully praying to get out of this with at least a shred of dignity. She asked if we would come with her. We were more than happy to follow her out of the restaurant, quickly! I thanked the waitress and bartender for their hearts to continue to help us search for the person and told them that Jesus loves them. We followed her up a few stores to an outside bungee jumping contraption. She introduced us to her friend and told him our story. I shared about my knee and filled in what she did not know. We asked if we could pray for his knee. He said, "Absolutely". I realized that we had entered into a teachable moment for my nieces as well as us, so I carefully followed my healing prayer team training and asked the man if we could lay hands on his shoulder, explaining that God could heal him whether we touched him or not. I did not want him to feel uncomfortable. He gave us the go ahead so I shared with my nieces that they could just hold hands with me if they wanted.

We prayed for an open heaven and thanked God that he hears our prayers and answers them! I do not believe that there is any one way to pray. Jesus offered a model in the Lord's Prayer that I believe gives glory to God but I do not think He intended it to be an ending but a beginning. A place to start, acknowledging God, declaring His holiness, and calling on His Kingdom to come on earth as it is in Heaven. It's a model. As we prayed, the Lord gave me a word of knowledge about the ligaments so I prayed healing over them. Matt prayed for his muscles to strengthen over the ligaments and Megan prayed that the pain would leave. By the time we all got done praying, including the young woman, the young man exclaimed that there was no more pain!

They shared with us that the doctor had said that his ligaments were torn and may never heal from all the continued stress on them. We were so excited about all of it!! We thanked both of them for letting us be a part of this. We shared that Jesus loved them and they said that they knew He did. WOW, it was really cool!! This was not my first journey in praying for healing, but it was the first time I got to share this level of prayer partnering with the Lord, with my nieces! I was stoked and on fire!! We thanked the Lord for His faithfulness and everything else we could think to thank Him for.

We headed back down the walkway to the van. We were all excited but walked in silence for a little while. Finally, out of nowhere, Leah said, "Well that was awkward"! We all burst out laughing. It was hilarious yet true at the same time. I shared with her that it was awkward for me too but if Jesus wants us to do something we should chance feeling awkward. I shared with them all the thoughts and fear going on inside me in the restaurant. I told them that I almost gave up a few times but felt like Jesus wanted them to be a part of this journey so that they would trust Him and take risks in the future. Taking the risk to be laughed at by people is worth it to get to experience the power that we have in the Holy Spirit through Jesus to love and to heal!! We were all pumped up and could not wait to get back to share it with our family. It was an amazing journey that we all got to share in which started with a cup of coffee. Think about that the next time you do not feel like going somewhere that your children want you to go with them!

Chapter 7

THIS PRESENT ONGOING JOURNEY

I have often felt the enemy pushing in as I stepped out more in my walk of faith. As you just heard the Mountain Top story, I almost gave up several times. Perhaps you have too. I have come to realize more and more that each new experience is the chance for us to be refined by God. No matter what we face, OUR GOD IS GREATER. I try not to give the enemy any glory or even a nod; I keep my eyes focused on Jesus. It is my hope that you have found the triumph and victory in Christ over the darkness. His promise that we are "more than conquerors in Him" is powerful. However, saying all that, I was not totally prepared for this new challenge! But as you will read, I have been so blessed by this season and thank God for the refining. It is always important to remember that no matter what happens, Christ's love cancels out all darts of the enemy if we walk by faith and wait for it! I am not saying that it will be all roses and sunshine, but if you keep your gaze focused on Jesus rather than the difficulty, you will find blessings beyond what you can imagine. Read on!!!

For years, I was fearful of failure which caused me at times to shrink away from success. I felt the enemy's hot breath on the back of my neck, always waiting for a chance to move in for the kill. 1 Peter 5:8(NIV) warns,

"Be alert and of sober mind. Your enemy the devil prowls around like a roaring lion looking for someone to devour."

As my focus shifted from giving Satan any glory to keeping my eyes fixed on Jesus, **I have learned to really appreciate seasons of trial**. It is one of these seasons that has prompted this book. I know, you have had to WAIT FOR IT for a while now!! I'm getting there. Since the day I wrote the check to take the Dayton School of Supernatural Ministry Class I have felt the atmosphere shift around me. Growing our faith muscle requires work. Challenges give us the opportunity to work those muscles. With this shift I have also felt an unseen resistance pressing me to remain depleted of identity living from an impoverished spirit rather than a royal princess heritage. I am not complaining because I know the end of the story! I know who wins and I really do love growing through what at times may seem like a hopeless situation! Romans 5:3-5 (NIV) contends that,

"Not only so, but we[a] also rejoice in our sufferings, because we know that suffering produces perseverance; perseverance, character; and character, hope. And hope does not put us to shame, because God's love has been poured out into our hearts through the Holy Spirit, who has been given to us."

I have always loved this verse and found great comfort in the fact that a life submitted to Christ gets the benefit and glory of His amazing love but also the chance to be refined! I love HOPE! I think it is by far one of the most amazing things that God gave us. Hope gives us the vision to look into the most tragic circumstance and see the promise of a new day dawning. The greatest hope we have as believers is the chance to live in eternity with Jesus because of His sacrifice! No greater love is this!!! No greater gift than to dwell in the house of the Lord forever.

Well, this story continues on August 30, 2013. I was scheduled for a routine mammogram. I have had them every year since I turned forty. This was suggested especially for women who have a history of cancer in their family, which I do. My mom had breast cancer and later died of bone marrow cancer. My grandmother on my dad's side also died of cancer. I have rebuked this generational curse and thanked God for a life free of cancer. I have always believed that I would not walk under this curse, meaning I would live out my days cancer-free.

Needless to say, I was greatly surprised to get the call from my doctor's office to say that the mammogram was suspicious and they were sending me for another mammogram and ultrasound. I remember telling my husband how interesting it was that I had physically moved during the particular x-ray where they said the suspect area was. I told him that I even mentioned it to the technician who assured me that all the pictures were fine. Since this was in the back of my head, I really did not think much of going for the ultrasound, that is, until I arrived at the appointment.

It was the afternoon of September 19th, 2013. DSSM had just begun on September 15th. I remember sitting out in the van praying for God's peace and comfort to fall on me. I suddenly felt alone, scared, and dejected. There was such an overshadowing of doom and gloom I felt as if I could not catch my breath. I had the sensation of drowning at the same time as being crushed by huge, deadly waves. I had not felt this way until arriving in the parking lot of the hospital where the office was located. Prayerfully looking back, it was revealed to me that I was sensing or discerning what so many women had felt before, having been given even worse news than I was about to receive. I have since prayed for that parking lot and hospital to be a place of comfort and peace. It truly felt like one of the lowest moments of my life. I would encourage you to go pray in any parking lot and building where people go to receive news and treatment of illnesses! Pray for everyone you can! The world needs more hope! Especially if you are someone who loves to pray but would never walk up to someone unknown and pray, this is non-threatening and needed greatly to shift the atmosphere in these places.

After quite a bit of prayer and worship, I finally felt calm enough to go into the office. Everyone was extremely nice. I sensed the technician who took me back for my mammogram was sad even though her cheery countenance would have not revealed this to everyone. I asked her if she was feeling fine. Tears welled up in her eyes as she expressed gratitude for my asking about her well-being. She shared with me the tumultuous last year of her life which included becoming a single mom. This is something that is near and dear to my heart. I have such compassion for single parents. I was one for a season of my life. It is not easy. The organization I founded, Assert Now, Inc. has a branch that is dedicated to working with single parents. It is important to have someone help you to navigate through these difficult circumstances and lead you to the greatest physician and psychologist – Jesus Christ.

Anyway, I felt such compassion and love for this young, courageous woman. I said a prayer and offered her my business card, telling her that I would love to have coffee and chat with her whenever she needed someone to be a non-biased listener. She was so appreciative. She gave me a huge hug before I left her office and was escorted to the next office for my ultrasound. I was so blessed to get to show love and kindness to this young woman. I mused that perhaps she was the reason for this journey. I was called to encourage and pray for a precious princess who needed words of kindness. With that thought, I dismissed any contemplation of worry. I have found that in serving others, there is such great joy and satisfaction. **Serving takes us outside of our own circumstance and carries us to a place of empathy into another's situation**. Perhaps that is one of the reasons why we are called to model Jesus who came to "serve and not be served!" **OUR FOCUS TURNS**

FROM INTERNAL TO EXTERNAL, FROM SELFISH TO SELFLESS.

After this warm and tender encounter, I was ushered into a room by another technician, and had quite the opposite of the tender moment I had just experienced. She was very matter-of-fact in her dialog and countenance. She asked me lots of questions about my medical history and if I had found the lump on my own. I told her that I had not found anything and asked was she sure there was one there. She did the ultrasound and for the first time, I felt the pain of a small lump. Tears welled up in me. I wanted to be a tough girl and prove to myself that I was not scared. I cried out to Jesus from the depths of my soul. I found my mind spiraling downward towards deep despair. Somewhere in the depth of my spirit I knew where this was headed. After I was finished, she gave me the directions outs of my next steps. She said that I had to have a biopsy to determine the nature of the lesion. She never specifically said that she felt it was cancerous, but I could discern that she felt that way.

I got dressed and left the office as quietly and quickly as possible without anyone noticing I was really upset. Who knows if I fooled any one? I can be a pretty good actress when I need to be and right then, for my own sanity, I needed to be at an Academy award winning level. I did not want anyone to ask me if I was okay because I knew I was barely holding it together. I got into the van and the floodgates opened up! I was so upset

I could not drive. Tears streamed down my face! All the worse, I could not get a hold of my husband Scott!

My mind raced. I did not want to call the boys and share this over the phone. Jesus just kept saying "Cry out to me", so I succumbed. Slowly and systematically, as I prayed and cried out, calm and comfort enveloped me. The peace that can only come from having a close and intimate relationship with Jesus Christ swept over me. It was then I knew that everything was going to be fine. Once I focused on Jesus, the ultimate source of peace, I was calm. I knew I would be okay in the waiting for it, the healing!

Once I finally spoke with Scott I felt even better about everything. I arrived home and we shared everything the technician had told me with the boys. I remember thinking that they must be in denial, because they were really not concerned. That in itself was a blessing because the enemy instantly showed me the pain and heartache they would go through if I had cancer, underwent the painful treatments, and ultimately died. I had to fight this thought the hardest. My mind reeled, **TAKE CAPTIVE MY THOUGTHS**! The battle was on! I sent out prayer requests to my many faithful warrior friends and family across the world, asking then to pray for miraculous healing and protection for my family! I also did not have insurance, so I asked for prayers for finances as well. Up until this point, the expenses were covered by a wellness fund through the doctor's office that performed the mammogram. I think it is amazing how they help women through these rough times! The fund, however, did not cover the next step, which was the biopsy, but they lovingly shared information about an organization I could call. It is funny now, looking back, we never questioned whether we should go through with the biopsy. We were just swept along in a river of a worldview that believed "this is the course you need to take". Looking back I did question if I should have done the biopsy.

While I awaited the paperwork to be able to proceed to the next step, some pretty amazing things happened. For one, I vowed to continue to be a powerful weapon of love in the Lord's army and not allow this new challenge to steal my joy or my testimony of His faithfulness. The song "While I'm Waiting" from the movie "Fireproof" began to take on a whole new meaning for me! If you have not heard it, I suggest you find it on YouTube. I have included the lyrics below to encourage you!

While I'm Waiting - John Waller / Metro Lyrics

I'm waiting; I'm waiting on You Lord
And I am hopeful; I'm waiting on You Lord
Though it is painful, but patiently I will wait

And I will move ahead bold and confident
Taking every step in obedience

While I'm waiting I will serve You

While I'm waiting I will worship
While I'm waiting I will not faint
I'll be running the race even while I wait

I'm waiting; I'm waiting on You Lord
And I am peaceful; I'm waiting on You Lord
Though it's not easy no, but faithfully I will wait
Yes, I will wait

And I will move ahead bold and confident
Taking every step in obedience

While I'm waiting I will serve You
While I'm waiting I will worship
While I'm waiting I will not faint
I'll be running the race even while I wait

I will move ahead bold and confident
I'll be taking every step in obedience, yeah

While I'm waiting I will serve You
While I'm waiting I will worship
While I'm waiting I will not faint

And I will serve You while I'm waiting
I will worship while I'm waiting
I will serve You while I'm waiting
I will worship while I'm waiting
I will serve You while I'm waiting
I will worship while I'm waiting on You Lord

I will serve You while I'm waiting
I will worship while I'm waiting
I will serve You while I'm waiting
I will worship while I'm waiting

Chapter 8

PLEASURE TO MEET YOU, ROBBY DAWKINS

Friday and Saturday, September 20th and 21st, 2013, were, admittedly, dark days for me. I rarely have had full-blown bad or dark days in my life. Even through sexual, physical, and emotional abuse, addictions, trafficking, failed relationships, and dismal financial times, I did not have full days of darkness. I walked through so many fires with the Lord that challenges became only momentary set-backs. Even when my mom died years ago (2001), there was a peace that came with it. I have had moments, ones that people have expressed should have sent me into a corner, balled up and paralyzed for weeks, but that is the grace of our Savior, I have always been able to cling to Him and find my footing fast! This time was more challenging; the enemy was hot on my trail speaking lies like, "God let you down, didn't He? You thought you would avoid cancer. Your sins have caused you this certain death"! These thoughts went on and on, as I spiraled into a deeper pit of despair.

Finally, after two days of allowing the enemy to be in my thoughts and life, I spilled my guts out to Scott, telling him all the wicked thoughts plaguing me. He was able to speak truth and pray for me. He reminded me that God loved me no matter what and that He has never let me down. This gave me GREAT peace and restored my usual joy and hope in the midst of hardship. It also marked a period where faith stories of the past (which will be shared later in the book), would be resurrected for my family as strength for the present battle! It also reminded me just how dark evil was and just how LOVING and KIND our Father, Son, and Holy Spirit are. God is not angry or hateful. God does not wish us harm or seek to punish us with disease or illness. If you feel this way, please find someone to speak truth and life to you.

THAT GOD WISHES HARM ON YOU, ME, OR ANYONE IS A LIE FROM THE PIT OF HELL.

His word is clear...He does not desire any to perish. He is slow to anger... Jonah 4:2 (NIV) says it best, *He (Jonah) prayed to the Lord, "Isn't this what I said, Lord, when I was still at home? That is what I tried to forestall by fleeing to Tarshish. I knew that you are a gracious and compassionate God, slow to anger and abounding in love, a God who relents from sending calamity.*

The context here is that Jonah (the prophet) did not want to prophecy what the Lord had told him because he knew that if Nineveh heard and repented, the Lord would not send calamity and Jonah may look like a fool. I love that! God warns His people and if they repent, He does not let the consequence of their sin, my sin fall. Does this sound like a God that condemns people with cancer? **NO NO NO**!! I truly hope that if you are facing anything like this or even worse, there is someone in your life to speak words of life and truth. And I truly pray from the deepest reaches of my spirit and soul that you feel comforted by Jesus.

Another thing that helped to put my focus back where it belonged, ON JESUS, was the speaker coming to our DSSM class on Sunday, September 22, 2013. I had seen Robby and heard some of the awesome testimonies of his life in "Furious Love" and "Father of Lights". I felt like this night the Holy Spirit was going to be unleashed in a new way! I had just barely begun reading Robby's book, "Do What Jesus Did" but already knew that I was reading the script of a kindred spirit! Robby is a risk taker too! I will not reveal too much of his book as I believe EVERYONE in the world should read it. Robby is authentic, funny, and powerful in faith. His love of life and people truly example someone who is trying to "DO WHAT JESUS DID"!

As Sunday night approached, I found the enemy sneaking back in, attacking with accusations of death and destruction. I felt tired and worn out. I could barely drag myself to the DSSM class. However, there was an excitement bubbling up that helped to fight the exhaustion because I knew that as hard as the enemy was trying to keep me from the class, he was scared of what Jesus was unleashing! This gave me the supercharge I needed to get up and get going! To keep my eyes fixed on Jesus and not what was physically going on around me!

One of my favorite parts of DSSM class is worship at the beginning. I love worship. I really try to submit my life in worship, whether work, leisure, prayer, music, it all goes to God. Colossians 3:23 has been a battle cry for me,

"Whatever you do, work at it with all your heart, as working for the Lord, not for men". Music has always been my single favorite way to offer praise to the Lord. When I was 5 years old, I wrote my first song called, "Thank You God". As only a five year old heart could rhyme:

Thank you God for the rivers so clear,
Thank you God for you being near
Thank you God for the grass and trees
Thank you for you being you and me being me!
Thank you God for my dad so strong
Thank you God that I belong
To a family full of love
Thank you God that you shine on us from above

Not a billboard hit or Dove award winner but the heart cry of a five year old who had been saved from a near death experience at age three. This story will be shared later in the book!

Worship at our church in is always powerful and I love to sing the Lord's praises with my fellow believers! It reminds me of being in the throne room singing, "Holy, Holy, Holy". This night, the Lord had a special treat for me. As I worshipped, swaying with the music, eyes closed and face lifted, lost in the sweet feeling of my Savior, I had a powerful vision.

Suddenly, from out of nowhere, I heard the sound of a mighty lion roar. It was so loud and fierce it made me shake! I tried to open my eyes to see where it was and it dawned on me that I was caught in an

encounter with my Abba Father! At first it startled me and took me a minute to regain my senses. The thought occurred to me that it reminded me of Aslan, in "Narnia" where He cries out in righteous indignation at the white witch's evil. After a few moments I realized I was seeing the Lion of Judah. I could sense His mighty presence, ominous and consuming. A Holy chill ran down my spine and God bumps broke out over my entire body. I was POSITIVE THAT THIS WAS THE LORD!! As I lifted my head to look at Him, his eyes pierced into my soul. I recognized those eyes as the ones who gazed at me as He handed me His heart. My body relaxed and peace flooded me. He suddenly, without warning, lunged forward. Though startled, I was not afraid. Viciously yet lovingly with the authority of the Lamb who conquered death, He bit the lesion from my body, spit it out, and emphatically faced me and declared, "It is finished. You are healed!" YEAH!! – THAT KNOCKED MY SOCKS OFF! I could feel tears streaming down my face. I thought this is what it must feel like when hot lava pours down the side of a volcano, burning everything in its path clearing the way for new life and vegetation to grow down the road. It was searing my cheeks, cleansing my soul, paving the way for the new life in me. The power of the vision was almost too much for me to bear. I mustered up the strength to cry out in my spirit and asked the Lord if this happened right now, if I was healed. Funny, I was not devastated or even upset by His response. It was simple yet held a weighty promise. He said, "No, not yet, but soon. Wait for it." He also said the enemy "Would not be permitted to take me out of the game!" His words were intentional and determined. I couldn't even grasp what this meant. I just wanted to receive the joy in this new promise!

WOW – After I really thought about it, quite honestly I was blown away! I had not even had my biopsy yet and the Lord had already promised healing! WHEW! I decided that I was going to hang on to this vision and word with everything I had! I was drawn back to the music and the worshippers around me. As we transitioned into the night, I quickly wrote every detail down so that I would not forget!

So this was how the night was going to unfold! Already God was bringing the Kingdom down in power! This was just a taste of what was to come! Robby brings a Holy presence with him; one of someone walking in the love and power of Christ. His passion for God's people, his inherited family was so strong. His message that the Lord moved on him to bring us was simple yet heavy-duty supercharged! **Satan and his workers are identity thieves**. Their mission is to undermine and destroy what the Lord wants to build up and send out. We should not fear this but stand firm on God's promises. Well, there you have it; I had just been given a wholehearted promise of a healing that still had not been fully diagnosed. I love how God moves in our lives if we allow Him! He knows all things before He creates them!

Robby went on to share that scripture promises that Jesus will never leave us or forsake us. The power of love and light, defeats the power of hate and darkness. One quote that Robby shared was, "**My gift to God is my AVAILABILITY, and God's gift to me is the ABILITY!**" Translation, we show up and the Holy Spirit does the work! He also shared a quote from John Wimber, "**You go and I (God) will show!**" It is so exciting to embrace the identity that we have in Christ. It is simple yet profound! We do nothing but receive from God, so that it may be poured out through our lives as we go and love for Jesus! One of the BIGGEST THINGS that Robby affirmed is that one of the definitions of **FAITH is RISK**.

All That Glitters

Okay, so if this night was not already phenomenal, the ending was like the grand finale at a fireworks display on the Fourth of July! As we went into a time of ministry, healing, and anointing after the teaching, someone yelled, "There is gold dust showing up". YEAH RIGHT!! I heard it and just as quickly dismissed it, lost in the sweet presence of the Holy Spirit. After what seemed like hours, I went back to my seat and relaxed into it looking at the stage/altar and all the people enjoying the presence of God. My son Matt was sitting there, so we began to share and process the night. He was equally as moved by Robby and what the Holy Spirit was doing! Okay now WAIT FOR IT!!! This is an absolutely true story!!

One of our friends returned to her seat with us and was flushed with excitement. She was thrusting her hands at us saying, "Look at my hands, look at my hands". It was **UNIMAGINABLE!** Her hands looked as if they were brushed with a bronzish gold dust. The tone of her skin resembled Jesus when He appeared to me in my encounters. I was so excited! I looked down at my own hands and realized that they were sprinkled with a very fine gold dust, twinkling in the dimly lit room. Matt looked down at his hands, and guess what????? **NOPE...A BIG FAT NOTHING.** As we looked at his hands, something incredible happened. White fine crystal looking dust started to appear right before our eyes. If all three of us had not been there together, we would not have believed it. Our friend had a word from the Lord that what her hands represented was what her resurrected body would look like in Heaven. **WOW...SHUT UP...REALLY!!!** That was confirmation and the explanation of why Jesus glowed in my encounters...It was His resurrected body and also, as I searched scripture for confirmation, it is the description of His resurrected body in the Bible! **This stuff is what movies are made of, yet there we were, sitting amidst the invasion, the impact of what happens when Heaven meets earth.**

Chapter 9

ON EARTH AS IT IS IN HEAVEN

During this time, I was the children's ministry director at a different church. I have always loved children and have been a powerful advocate for them throughout my life! On Wednesday nights we had a program that was called "Ignite". The mission: to ignite the hearts of the children to have a passionate relationship with Christ, and from that, to share His love with others. Over the past few years we had been teaching the children how to hear God's voice through His word and through the power of the Holy Spirit within all of us. We had so much fun with this. One of our favorite chants was "There is no junior Holy Spirit"! For fun, we would pray and invite the junior, senior-citizen, young adult and middle aged Holy Spirit into the room. They would love to yell, "NO!" **I would then ask them who we should invite and they would again shout, "The Holy Spirit! We all have the same spirit in us!"** How powerful is that! If children learn that they are powered by the same Holy Spirit as adults, they are unstoppable for the Lord. To substantiate this truth, let me share a story about this love and power available to them, to you, to me, to all who are in Christ.

It was Wednesday, September 25, 2013. I was ablaze after hearing Robby Dawkins speak again on taking risks and not giving up! I could not wait to share some of the stories with the children that he had shared with us. Matt was one of our leaders, but he could not come that particular night because he had taken a friend to the hospital with a swollen leg that had been festering from an injury a month earlier. He texted me from the hospital and asked to have the kids pray for healing because the doctors had determined that he had several blood clots in his leg and was at serious risk and in grave danger. After the children arrived we spent some time reading scripture and putting on the armor of God. We prayed fervently for Matt's friend who is also a fellow brother in Christ to us all. After prayer, I was bursting with excitement to share about my week!

I could not wait to tell them about Sunday night and the power of God's presence manifesting in gold dust. For me, one of the most exciting parts of the story was that the three of us who had the gold dust experience were currently the teachers with this group of children. The kids were amazed and supercharged over the testimony. Kids are so pure and simple. They believe truth so easily. Kids also can detect a phony, authenticity with them is important, as it is with all people.

I began to then recount Robby's teaching on the dominion we have over the earth given at creation that we can read in Genesis. They embraced that without hesitation! They started proclaiming healing over the blood clots again, declaring passionately, "In Jesus' name". They asked the Holy Spirit to come in power and dissolve the blood clots. They prayed with a ferocity and authority that could only have manifested through the Holy Spirit's presence. It was very moving for me. I found it hard to stand in the overwhelming presence and power of the spirit. I am sure that God, who delights in His children, was rejoicing at the sight. When our prayer time ended, we had to go meet the younger group. We gathered everything to transition to the next room.

When we went into meet with them, one of the leaders said, "We need to pray for one of the children present. He is six years old..." Before she could finish, a couple of the children came up to me yelling and pulling on me, "Miss Aurora, Miss Aurora, we have to pray for our friend! He is covered in hives and wants us to pray for him!"

FIRST, LET ME SAY THAT IF YOU HAVE NEVER HAD THE CHANCE TO PRAY WITH CHILDREN, DO IT!! THEIR SIMPLE FAITH WILL MELT YOUR HEART, AND IT WILL STOP THE ENEMY IN HIS TRACKS! JESUS IS VERY CLEAR ABOUT HOW HE FEELS ABOUT CHILDREN.

In Matthew 19:14, Jesus said, "Let the little children come to me, and do not hinder them, for the kingdom of heaven belongs to such as these."

ALSO, IF YOU HAVE EVER DIMINISHED THESE PRECIOUS WARRIORS AS ONLY CUTE AND HARMLESS CHILDREN WHEN THEY

PRAYED, BE AWARE THAT LIONS ARE CUTE AS CUBS TOO BUT CAN STILL DO GREAT DAMAGE!! THERE IS NO JUNIOR HOLY SPIRIT!! CHILDREN WHO UNDERSTAND THIS ARE GREAT WEAPONS AGAINST THE ENEMY!!!

We loved to pray **His kingdom come, on earth as it is in heaven**! Jesus says it belongs to the children, they should know the power of love and authority they have within it!

To continue, they started dragging me into the room and were already putting a chair in the middle of the floor for the child to sit down so we could pray. One of the leaders explained that his mom said she had been at the hospital all day long with him and they could not figure out anything other than it was some form of allergic reaction. Now, I know what you are thinking, first of all, why is he here? What if he was contagious and the doctors were wrong? **Okay, well I thought it too.** His mom said that he had really wanted to come to class tonight for prayer so she had brought him. Now I have to admit, when I saw him I was a little taken aback. His arms and legs were covered with red irritation and there were white and red welts in several places. If someone had asked me to lay hands on him at that moment, I hate to admit my humanness but, I probably would have been a little resistant **– it looked that bad!**

Thank God that the children are little kingdom sponges and fearless! We started praying for the Holy Spirit to come in power. We prayed an open heaven over the room. The young man confirmed that he wanted prayer so we sat him in the chair and circled around him. The children started praying and the Holy Spirit fell so powerfully that they were exclaiming, "My hands are feeling hot and I think that I should touch his leg". Again, I am not so sure I would have been able to act on this prompting of the Spirit and reach out and touch him. I suggested the children follow the Spirit's leading as long as he agreed. One of the boys placed his hand on the worst spot on his friend's leg and started proclaiming, "Spots go and leg be healed in Jesus' name!" I suggested that they keep proclaiming "More Lord, more Lord" until the healing was complete. They continued to pray with such power and boldness it brought tears to my eyes. As we watched and prayed, his welts began to leave right before our very eyes and the redness was gone. The children were giddy with the excitement of it all and the power of the presence of the Holy Spirit! IT WAS AWESOME!! It truly was miraculous to watch! WOW – I just love how God honors the promises He has given us in His word! It got better and better because the more his spots decreased the more intentional and excited their prayers were.

When his mom showed up, we brought her in to show her and share what had happened. Tears started to spill from her eyes as she saw her little angel's arms and legs healed!! She then went to her son so excited and hugged him. He looked at her and she exclaimed, "Oh my goodness, his face isn't swollen anymore either!" We didn't even realize his face had been swollen but his mom did. This just heaped glory upon glory on the situation. We all joined in to praise the Lord for this healing.

Right after that, Matt came in from taking his friend to the hospital. He told us that they were keeping his friend overnight for observation but the pain had stopped and the clot was not as serious as they had originally diagnosed. They felt he was "out of the woods" as far as danger went! Of course we knew this was the Holy Spirit's healing power from the precious prayers of the children! The kids were so excited that Jesus saved Matt's friend too!

I followed up with the boy's mom the next morning. She said that his arms and neck were completely clear. She also said his chest and stomach were still very red and itching and asked if we would continue to pray. The children could not see his chest and stomach so they did not pray for that. **While we know that our God could have healed that too, it was another good lesson for them in praying for the unseen!** I told her that I was going to send the prayer request out to some of the child prayer warriors right away. I shared it with a few of the moms whose children had prayed the night before. I also posted it on our DSSM Facebook page. By 4:00pm she called me very elated to share that he was completely healed! God is GREAT!

On Sunday I shared with the children the continuing story about their friend's stomach and praying for the entire body. They were very excited to hear that Jesus had fully healed him. We discussed the importance of listening to the voice of the Lord/Holy Spirit when praying for healing. The children had prayed for what they could see but the Spirit knew what they could not see. After I shared this with them, three of the children said that they thought about praying for his stomach but did not know if they should or not. We talked about praying for it even if they did not know if it hurt or had difficulty. Their little sponge receptors were soaking every last drop of the lesson up for another day! They really do embrace the idea that the same spirit lives in them! Say it with me, "**THERE IS NO JUNIOR HOLY SPIRIT**"! Now teach the power to a child in your life!

After our talk, they were all so anxious to pray for someone, anyone, so they could listen and hear from the Holy Spirit instead of just seeing with their eyes! <u>**I love how children will automatically test to see if what you tell them is true**</u>. God's word calls us all to, "*Test and approve His good, pleasing, and perfect will for our lives.*" (Romans 12:2) Instilling scripture and the testing of His Word early is so important for children, so that they experience John 8:32, "*Then you will know the truth, and the truth will set you free.*" The enemy will try to twist and steal truth but once scripture is planted and the seeds take root, there is nothing stopping them! The children had many more chances to practice what they learned.

Chapter 10

ANOTHER VISION

After church it was extremely difficult leaving the atmosphere of the presence of God in the children's room. To make it worse, as I walked out many people came to ask questions about my suspect lesion. It had only been a few days since my ultrasound. I still had not been set up for an appointment for my biopsy. The biggest question coming from both my extended biological and church family was, "**WHEN would I have the biopsy?**"

We had no idea when the biopsy would be scheduled yet there was a strong peace that the Lord was walking us through this! It had been covered in prayer so we were waiting. Since we did not have insurance for me, I had to be scheduled when all the paperwork went through with the organization that was going to fund my biopsy. Physically, emotionally, and spiritually depleted from the events of the morning and the multitude of questions, I went home to rest before DSSM class.

I was looking forward to my Sunday night DSSM class this week, September 29, 2013! I always feel the Lord very strongly as I have a very intimate relationship with him. It is hard to imagine it being even stronger but music worship always makes my time with Him seem supercharged. God met me every week in such a powerful way. All I could think was, "I want more Lord, more of what I had this past week"! Worship was once again powerful and the Holy Spirit filled the room, His presence was so overwhelming that I had to sit down before I fell down! And...As I sat there, captivated by His presence:

Jesus appeared before me! He was almost floating or hovering just above the ground. Light rays were shooting out of His body like lightning, but it was a continuous pulsing, not in flashes. He reached out His hand and touched His finger, which was glowing, to the spot where the lesion showed up on the ultrasound. In an instant the ball exploded into millions of tiny light particles and was absorbed in the atmosphere. He again told me that it was finished and that the enemy would not be allowed to "TAKE ME OUT OF THE GAME". I really began to pray about this word that He gave me for a second time, "The enemy would not be allowed to take me out of the game." What did this mean? That I would not die? That it would not be cancerous? The questions swirled until I was once again aware of the music.

CANCER – The word itself strikes fear in so many. I lost both my grandmother and mother to cancer, so I knew the ravages of its affliction. This demon was not going to strike fear in my heart. Whether I live 2 minutes or another 200 years, I will keep my eyes focused on Jesus! I was going to trust God with my life as He has proven faithful through the years!!!

I quickly wrote down the vision so that I would not forget the details, and the powerful feeling of healing that came with it. Tonight was a live speaker so I had to write quickly so that I did not miss the presentation!

I cannot remember the whole story that the teacher shared about the miraculous healing of an inoperable brain tumor. I do know that as she shared it, the Lord reminded me of both of the powerful visions He had given me. I felt such love and peace well up inside of me. I sensed He was saying, "WAIT FOR IT…Wait on me, I am faithful!" My family and I continued to stand in agreement with what The Lord had shown me; waiting to see what would happen next as the journey continued to unfold. One of the scriptures shared this night was:

Joshua 1:9 (NIV), *"Have I not commanded you? Be strong and courageous. Do not be afraid; do not be discouraged, for the Lord your God will be with you wherever you go."*

This verse had become a battle cry for my life before they shared it, so their word was a confirmation for me. The more I abided (spending quiet time just with Jesus) and stepped out and took **RISKS,** to pray for people, the closer I drew to Him for strength and wisdom. It is impossible to walk radically with Jesus without having an intimate relationship with Him! There is a huge sense of strength and courage which comes from faith in Him! It is the greatest feeling and joy I have every felt in my life. The great news is it is not fleeting but always present and available – we just have to engage!

The Armor of God was another scripture that was shared:

Ephesians 6:10-18(NIV) *"Finally, be strong in the Lord and in his mighty power. Put on the full armor of God, so that you can take your stand against the devil's schemes. For our struggle is not against flesh and blood, but against the rulers, against the authorities, against the powers of this dark world and against the spiritual forces of evil in the heavenly realms. Therefore put on the full armor of God, so that when the day of evil comes, you may be able to stand your ground, and after you have done everything, to stand. Stand firm then, with the **belt of truth buckled** around your waist, with the **breastplate of righteousness** in place, and with your **feet fitted with the readiness that comes from the gospel of peace**. In addition to all this, take up the **shield of faith**, with which you can extinguish all the flaming arrows of the evil one. Take the **helmet of salvation** and the **sword of the Spirit**, which is the word of God. And pray in the Spirit on all occasions with all kinds of prayers and requests. With this in mind, be alert and always keep on praying for all of the Lord's people.*

This is one of my favorite scriptures because of the power it holds. That night, the Lord revealed through the teacher an even greater perspective for me. Remember in the beginning of this book we discussed perspective? Well, this perspective shift that the Lord was giving me through the supernatural ways He had been showing up brought about a new level of power and confidence in walking with Jesus.

She said that the armor was made of iron; she further explained that it was like how Margaret Thatcher (Past Prime Minister of Great Britain and a powerful lady) was called the Iron Lady meaning she was "RESOLUTE". Unshakeable and unwavering are the two definitions I liked the most (Google Web Definitions). She went on to share other definitions from Webster's dictionary: not yielding, determined, fixed for a purpose, and great strength. This showed me just how impenetrable this armor is making it even more important to remember to put it on and keep it on for protection! Walking with this armor makes us impenetrable!

If you are a parent and have not equipped yourself and your children with God's armor, I encourage you to pray it on every day. Some people believe that you do not need to pray it on every day. For me, it is a fresh impartation each day and reminder of each piece and what it represents. **TRUTH ALWAYS, LIVING RIGHTLY, PEACE IN ALL CIRCUMSTANCES, FAITH, OUR MIND SET ON CHRIST, AND GOD'S WORD!!** If you have children, try putting on imaginary armor with them daily as you begin each day. They will love it and never forget it. This will instill scripture and the Lord's promise of protection. It will also be a legacy to the generations after you are gone!

Needless to say I prayed the armor of God and many other scriptures over me. This came in very handy the day I finally went for my biopsy!

Chapter 11

THE DAY OF TRUTH

October 15th, 2013 arrived with great joy and great trepidation. My biopsy appointment was scheduled for 7:15 am. Scott went with me to the medical center where the procedure was to take place. I was actually feeling really good! Peace and joy bubbled up from deep within me. I had a word from the Lord that I needed to pray with the nurses who took care of me so I had a mission in all of this, which always excites me! As I've shared before, it also takes the focus off of me and my challenges. I knew that God was calling me into a deeper understanding of faith and love; I was just not sure how it would play out. Waiting for it and walking in faith, particularly with radical faith, is never easy for those around you. I know, that I know, that I know, deep within me when the Lord is directing me on a path, but many times others are not so sure. In this journey it has been such a blessing that Matt and Clint also believe in this faith walk along with Scott and me! There is great strength you draw when your immediate family is in agreement.

We were met by a sweet receptionist named Joy. Only a God like ours would place a precious lady who loved Him and was named Joy in the room for me to meet that day! I will never forget her! She and I instantly connected. While we chatted and she searched for my paperwork, it became apparent that there was some confusion. She called the other organization that was funding my biopsy to have them fax exactly what was needed to ensure that we did not miss our appointment. I could sense Joy was feeling a bit frazzled. She maintained her composure but I could still feel the rippling of difficulty. She quietly shared that she needed some prayer for a situation that was currently happening in the office. I quietly prayed over her. You could feel the power of the Holy Spirit in the room and the peace that descended upon everyone. For me there was a great feeling of comfort as I was able to forget about my own situation and was able to put another's worries above my own. At that moment all I could think about was praying with and for this precious sister's difficulty.

IF YOU ARE WORRYING ABOUT SOMETHING RIGHT NOW, PLEASE TAKE A BREAK FROM READING AND FOCUS ON THE LORD. ASK HIM WHO HE WANTS YOU TO PRAY FOR. I AM SURE THERE ARE SEVERAL PEOPLE YOU KNOW WHO COULD USE YOUR PRAYER. IF YOU CANNOT THINK OF ANY, OR NONE ARE REVEALED TO YOU, PRAY FOR ME!! I CAN ALWAYS USE PRAYER! THIS IS SO EMPOWERING BECAUSE IT REALLY DOES TAKE YOUR MIND OFF YOUR WORRIES AND PUTS YOUR FOCUS BACK ON JESUS.

It was finally time for me to be called back. Scott was not permitted to come back with me. They preferred for him to wait in the waiting room. I was fine with this as I still felt an urgency to pray with the nurses and knew that they may feel more comfortable with just us women in the room. Once I was changed and in the room, there were two nurses there to help prep for the doctor to perform the biopsy. At this point I would like to segue and share some healthy counsel to women who have been through this.

PLEASE DO NOT TELL OTHER WOMEN FACING BIOPSIES OR SURGERIES YOUR HORROR STORIES. IT JUST MAKES THEM WORRY AND FRET! EVEN THE STRONGEST WOMEN OF FAITH WILL BE SHAKEN! INSTEAD, PRAY WITH THEM AND GIVE THEM WORDS OF ENCOURAGEMENT!! NOBODY BENEFITS FROM NEGATIVITY! AND DON'T TELL ME YOU ARE JUST BEING HONEST; I BELIEVE THAT IS AN EXCUSE TO SPEW NEGATIVITY! HONESTLY, YOU HAVE NO CLUE WHAT IS GOING TO HAPPEN WITH THIS PERSON OR THEIR SITUATION. GOD IS A BIG GOD AND CAPABLE OF ANYTHING, SO WHY BE A DEBBIE DOWNER FOR THEM!

Yes, I have been the victim of tales of biopsy horrors. My mom used to say that the road to hell is paved with good intentions. I would have to agree in this case. I know well-meaning, good intentioned people who have no idea the damage they are doing when sharing the gory details of their journey. Of course, I chose to listen so that makes me a willing party. I will say that it only took a few stories for me to draw boundaries and kindly suggest that they not share the details but instead pray for a blessed time during my biopsy. **The truth is, I would prefer to just trust God to lead me through trials.**

Before we started, I asked the two ladies in the examination room if I could pray with them. One eagerly said yes, and the other agreed but did not seem very amiable. After praying, the spirit was heavy in the room and the lady who was not amiable seemed more carefree and light hearted. Thank you Jesus! After lying down on the exam table and receiving instruction on the procedure, the sonogram to locate the lump (lesion) began. When the technician found the intruder, I had an overwhelming sense to ask her to pray healing for it.

So I jumped in with both feet and asked her if she believed in Jesus. She said yes and that she was a Christian. I asked her if she believed that Jesus could heal me right now. She said yes. I asked her if she realized that she could command the lump to be gone in Jesus name and it could be gone. She said......nothing. I asked her if she understood that being a Christian gave her the power and authority through Jesus over sickness, demons, and death. She muttered a half-hearted yes. I asked her if she would like to try it with me helping her to see how easy it was. I explained to her that it was about Jesus and not whether she "could" do it or not. I was not concerned about the outcome as I know my Redeemer loves me and the promises I have received! She agreed. So I talked her through it. First we thanked God for hearing us. I told her to command the lump to be gone in Jesus name. She meekly mumbled the words. I told her to do it again but this time to do it with confidence believing that **WITH GOD ALL THINGS ARE POSSIBLE**. She prayed again with a renewed confidence. Just as she began to relocate the lesion, the door creaked open and the moment was gone. I thanked her for her bold courage! I have since prayed that she has had the courage to pray for others who came after me. What a POWERFUL MINISTRY opportunity for those in health care. **It does not negate doctors or their importance but it does bring the ultimate healer into the process!**

The doctor arrived, so that meant it was time for the procedure to begin, because the lump had not disappeared with the prayer. I am not going to share any details here accept to say that it was not at all like the horrors that I had heard. I would not say it was fun by any means, but it was not as bad as childbirth either.☺ As I lay there, I was reminded of a word God had spoken to me, over and over again.

I WILL NOT ALLOW THE ENEMY TO TAKE YOU OUT OF THE GAME.

This word from God, that I was not going to be taken out of the game, continued to play like a broken record in my mind. My thoughts continually screamed, what does that mean Lord, what does that mean? Of course praying and discerning what this means in my life was a whole other issue. So I began praying earnestly for an answer. Remember, when I heard this I had not even had a biopsy, so the prospect that the biopsy could come back benign still remained in the realm of possibilities!

However, I truly had a sense that the biopsy was going to come back as malignant. I felt that this would be an integral part of the mission I have been called to in my life; another time where I would be challenged to trust God in spite of the overwhelming difficulty. Of course, I still had that ever present, annoying voice in my head that wanted to ask, "What did I do wrong, Lord? Have I not been faithful to trust you and obedient to walk where you lead me?" I knew that this battle would continue and I would continue to fight with His mighty weapons of warfare. It does seem as though these onslaughts are coming less and less and last only a fraction of time. It does not take me long to readjust my sights on God's sovereignty and amazing grace in my life and continue to WAIT FOR IT and walk by faith!

I have always found good out of seemingly "bad" circumstances in my life! I sincerely believe that there is a greater good that is coming from this, one even bigger than just growing my faith. John Dickson, in <u>Worship Warrior</u> states, "But it wasn't always a matter of what I had done wrong; it was a matter of what the Lord was building in me…Our praise cannot be limited to our mountaintop experiences. It must be tested in the valley (p. 61)". This was certainly a valley season so I was going to make sure that there was fruit from it! As I and several accountability prayer warriors prayed, the overwhelming sense was that the Lord had already given a promise of radical healing through His power and not by earthly means so this was the direction to continue to place unwavering faith.

Chapter 12

RADICAL FAITH

As I have already shared, radical faith is something that is part of my DNA. **It is important to share that I do not just decide to do radical things and then pray that they work out. I only radically walk where the Lord calls me, which is why it is easy for me to stand in faith during times of testing!** I have dozens and dozens of stories where there has been a step out in faith and then an amazing blessing and fruit from the obedience! I am going to share one right now that is directly connected to this present faith journey! I am also only going to share a very small part of the whole story. This segment is just a quick overview of three days of this journey.

It was Thursday, August 16th, 2012. A team of five of us was headed to Poland on a mission trip partnering with a Christian ministry in Warsaw. We were going to assist with a children's sports camp at their Christian camp in Zakosciele. We headed to the airport fully loaded with our luggage, passports, team, and no tickets. **THAT'S RIGHT, I SAID NO TICKETS!** Our entire team had prayed and for months tried to raise funds, with only half of the provision coming in that was needed for the journey. Since each one of us had a separate encounter with God and believed that He had called us to go to Poland, we did the only thing we could think of, go to the airport, WAIT FOR IT, and pray. We did not know how God was going to meet the need of 5 international tickets but we knew He would because He promised. One day turned into three days. We did not spend the night there but we started at 8am each day and left at 4pm. The last day we sat there, we left at 3pm because the flight we needed was leaving so we knew that we were not flying out Saturday. By now, we all were pretty discouraged. Everyone but Scott and I decided to go out and shake off the disappointment by visiting family and friends. Up until now, the team had stayed at our house as if we were already gone. At this point, unlike the rest of the team, I did not want to see anyone because many of our family and friends, most of whom are fellow believers in Christ, were beginning to share through texts, emails, and phone calls that perhaps we should give up and realize we were wrong and had not heard God correctly.

WHAT!!!!! THAT'S RIGHT, YOU READ IT, THIS WAS ABSOLUTELY PART OF OUR JOURNEY, DISCOURAGEMENT AND DEFEAT FROM FAMILY, FELLOW BROTHERS AND SISTERS IN FAITH!!!!!

Unfortunately I see this happen over and over again with people rooted in Christianity. Few want to WAIT FOR IT, the promise or blessing to manifest.

I just wanted to cry out in the privacy of our home to God. Perhaps there was the humiliation of being wrong looming in the air, that human sense of pride that I did not want to look stupid, or perhaps just the necessity or the desire to lick my wounds in private. After all, I was the one who originally heard from the Lord and was the team leader. I was the one who was responsible for any disaster that happened, right? As we sat in our home, I began to question if I had heard correctly. The banter went something like, "Oh God, how could I have heard so wrongly? I usually hear you so well. I really messed up and lead everyone down a dark path! They will never trust me again!" It droned on and on for what seemed like hours. My pity party and despair was making me sick to my stomach. I needed intervention!

Scott, who is very grounded in reality, had heard from God very clearly some months back and was sure that we had heard correctly. Now this was big because Scott does not believe that he hears from God very much. He gently reminded me that we just had to remain faithful and WAIT FOR IT. He knew and believed we had both heard very clearly! I knew he was right. It was the intervention and conviction that I needed! I hit the floor crying in repentance for wavering in my faith. The tears spilled out all over the floor as I cried out, as an animal caught in a vicious trap with steel teeth tearing at my flesh, for comfort and release. I wailed and asked for forgiveness for not trusting that God would remain faithful even when I was not remaining faithful to His promise. I was truly a tormented soul at that point, feeling the weight of disappointment upon my shoulders. Once it was all out and I just lay on the floor exhausted, something amazing happened, the phone rang.

The phone ringing in itself is not amazing, and the way I was feeling it may have been tragic, but somewhere deep within I felt compelled to answer it immediately. I looked and recognized the name; I showed Scott and he nodded, affirming that I should answer it. The voice on the other end (wishing to remain anonymous to the world) started out by apologizing profusely for not calling sooner. They said that they were told by God, hours earlier that day, to give us the rest of the money we needed to go to Poland! What, are you playing a joke? We needed $4000! This was incredible! There is more to this story but you get the point! We had indeed heard correctly and just needed to WAIT FOR IT and remain faithful. Needless to say, we went to Poland. This journey has not only grown our faith, but also for many around the world who know us, and lived it with us! This incredible faith journey would become a rock the Lord gave us to cling to in the seasons and trials ahead.

Live By Faith and Not By Sight

I wish I could tell you that the lump was benign. Of course, I probably would not be writing now if it had been. The day after the biopsy, I got a phone call from a very abrupt young woman telling me that my surgery would not be covered by the organization who had paid for the biopsy procedure. I was a little confused since I was told by my doctor that it would take two to three days for results and this was less than 24 hours. I explained to her, thinking that she was confused, that it was already paid for, assuming she was talking about the biopsy the day before. She was quite curt again and gave me the name of the hospital that I could call to try and get help with funding for my surgery. I prayed for her in my spirit. It must be hard to do her job. Remember, I did not have health insurance throughout this, so that part she had correct, I did need help with the financing if I was going to have further medical procedures, which as of yet, had not even been verified.

After I hung up, I was pretty upset. I asked a pastor I worked with to pray with me. He knew I was rattled so we prayed and I felt somewhat comforted. Truthfully, even though I believed she already had the results and I knew that they were not the results I would like to have, I knew they were the results that I WOULD have.

I tried to make sense of her call by contacting my doctor, the biopsy surgery center, and my husband. When I finally received a call back from my doctor hours later, he asked me to come in for an appointment the next day so we could try and figure this out. It was done. The pit in my stomach grew. I knew that he already had the results and they were not good. He denied knowing the results but I knew he was not going to chance telling me anything over the phone that may be devastating. As a counselor, I understand that you never know how someone will react to "bad" news so I, myself, would have waited until I could speak to my client face to face, especially when sharing something that could ultimately be life altering like a diagnosis of cancer.

You could almost hear the military band playing "Taps" as we went to my doctor's office. Everyone was cheerfully courteous, as usual, they were not "overly nice" because they think you are dying, so that was refreshing as I had faced that so many times from people who knew I was going for a biopsy! We were ushered into one of the back examination rooms. When the doc came in, he was compassionate and gentle as he, in detail, explained the findings of the biopsy. In short, there was a lesion on my duct, in my right breast that was labeled as carcinoma. He explained that this would be removed surgically and that a biopsy would also be taken of my lymph node to ensure that the malignancy was isolated to the breast. He also shared that there could be chemotherapy and/or radiation as a follow up. He offered that if the cancer had not spread to lymph nodes or other areas, the surgery may be sufficient. This he shared was the good news. Yeah right! I was not feeling it at the moment.

I kept a positive demeanor, so far feeling calm and composed. I shared the visions I had of supernatural healing and the belief that our family had for a miracle in this situation. While he was sensitive to our belief, we could tell that he did not share the same hope or vision. He promoted the idea of surgery and gave me the phone number to the surgical team he thought we should use. It's funny; I felt complete peace in the office. I had already been prepared for the news. While the size and severity of the diagnosis have seemed minimal, it was still a threat to my body and health. However, I felt very blessed that I did not receive worse news! We thanked him and left the office. When we stepped outside the building, an extreme sickness hit the pit of my stomach and my mind began to swirl. Oh no, here they came again, those crushing thoughts of death and destruction! There was no way I could stand the thought of dying before my boys, particularly Clint, was grown.

So many thoughts came crashing in! The boys, Scott, my ministries, my extended family, and the spiral went further and further down into the pit of despair. Thankfully it was only momentary and the Lord snapped me out of it and back to my always present faith and trust that God has "plans to prosper me and not to harm me, plans for a future" (Jeremiah 29:11). No matter what the next days, weeks, months, and years held, I could be sure that God's plans are greater and more complete than mine! I honestly do not know what I would do if I did not have the comfort of knowing Jesus so intimately. There are many who think this is just weak philosophy designed to avoid the severity of life. Well let me assure you that I lived for a long period with that same belief that it was weak philosophy. Life then was difficult and much of the time hopeless!

We went home and sat down and talked with Matt and Clint. I told them that the doctor wanted me to go have a surgery consultation and we all prayed for the Lord to lead us in the direction we should go. We did not have what we felt was a definitive answer so we decided to make the appointment with the surgeon and hear what he had to say. It took me a few more days to make the appointment with the surgeon. His receptionist was another quite curt woman who emphatically informed me that my consultation would cost a few hundred dollars and it was payable at the time of the consultation. We did not have that amount of money set aside but I knew that there would be family and friends willing to help if we needed finances! At this point though, I felt very frustrated and sorry for the two abrupt women I had encountered. I began to pray for both of them. As I prayed, I felt a swell of compassion go out for them. The words of knowledge that swept over me from the Lord were, "It must be hard to work in these environments and constantly see women in serious health danger yet no budget for the procedures. You must have to steel yourself against the pain of these women". The Lord showed me that this could be the reason that these two women seemingly lacked compassion or sensitivity to the plight. It was a defense mechanism. I decided to schedule the appointment knowing that the funds had not been secured yet.

After I made the appointment, it did not sit well with my soul. I sat our family back down and shared with them that I did not have peace about even going to the consultation. Almost in unison, Scott, Matt, and Clint shared that they were in agreement. It was at this point that we fully committed to WAIT FOR IT and walk in the faith healing that God had already shown me no matter how it played out! We had the tough talk once again that if I die tomorrow, we are going to stand firm in belief that it was God's plan for my life and that a greater plan would be unfolding in the process. We discussed the Poland trip where in the end, if you remember; people were saying we must not have heard from God correctly. I say NO, we just have to trust His plan and WAIT FOR IT to unfold even though we may not like what we are hearing or what is happening. Little did we understand at the time of our Poland mission trip that the journey of faith would be replayed over and over again through this new faith walk. There was the constant reminder that if we wait on the Lord, HE IS FAITHFUL, and His plans are the BEST!!!! My life verse has always been:

Isaiah 40:31, "Those who wait (hope) in the Lord will renew their strength, they will run and not be weary, they will walk and not be faint, they will mount up with wings like eagles!"

It is funny how it truly matches the path of my life. I have waited on the Lord for many things that have yet to manifest in my life. I truly believe that this is another amazing adventure that we will look back on with awe and thankfulness. Another big thing I have waited on is a recurring dream I had since I was 14 years old. The dream was so vivid, clear, and directional, that I knew it was prophetic for my life. At the writing of this book so far, I am 52 years old and it has not occurred. This, 38 years later, I am still waiting and believing God that this dream will manifest physically in my life. Let me share it.

In my dream, suddenly I was on a path, like a deer path, thin and beaten down to the earth. It was so narrow that I could barely keep both feet on the path without walking one foot in front of the other. I was sandwiched between a long line of bodies all belonging to an African tribe. We trudged up the mountain single-file on the path that skirted along the edge. I was the only woman and only Caucasian in the group. I remember feeling somewhere deep in my soul the safety and comfort of being in this group, as if it was so natural and exactly where I belonged. There was a gentle breeze that blew the grasses along the mountain; with it came a peace yet excitement for the journey. I remember thinking that the mountain we were on was Kilimanjaro. (I have no idea why I thought that because I had never even seen Kilimanjaro much less knew where it was) As we progressed, the sun moved to an overhead position, beating down on us. Interestingly, we were not hot because the breeze, which was surprisingly cool, refreshed us as we moved along silently. It was just the perfect temperature and day!

The leader, whom we called the Holy Man, fell back from the lead position and came to slowly walk at my side. His sandals made a swishing sound as he walked in the tall, wispy grass that lined the edge of the path. He was a little taller than me and wore a bright gold, yellow, orange, and blue striped shirt that was longer than most typical American shirts and hung loosely on his body. Ahead on the right was a grass and stick hut. It was rounded and woven together with what looked like the gray moss that hangs off of trees in the south part of the United States. There was a door on it also made of the brush from the mountain and it swung to the rhythm of the breeze. There was smoke curling from the top of the roof, where a hole was to vent the hut. It was like something out of a cartoon, appearing almost surreal. As we approached, the Holy Man quietly said that I was supposed to go in and pray with him. His words resonated with what I had already sensed; I knew in my spirit that he was correct. I was compelled to go in with him. There was something, a truth that I was supposed to find inside the thatched walls. As we entered, we encountered the delicious smell of sweet grass and the overwhelming presence of God. We sat quietly for a few minutes and he began to pray in his native tongue. As he prayed I heard the Lord tell me that He was sending me to the African nation to share His love with them. He showed me great multitudes that I would speak to and would come to know Jesus Christ through the simple yet powerful testimony of my life. When I awoke from the dream I could still smell the sweet grass lingering in the air. It took a few minutes to fully emerge from the encounter. Once I was fully cognizant, I knew that it had been a very real encounter. This dream recurred several times throughout the years.

If God gave me the gift of faith to believe and still wait on this dream to come true after 35 plus years, then surely I could wait on healing. I have truly found in this life that waiting on the Lord works if we are patient for His timing to manifest and not rush based on our own timing! Like Job, over and over again I am reminded that there will be naysayers and negative Nate's and Nellie's (if this is your name, I am sorry I am not targeting anyone in particular, just men and women alike) along the way. It is my/your job to keep our eyes and thoughts fixed on the God things and not allow distraction or discouragement by anything else. This would prove to be hard as my health journey continued.

Chapter 13

WALK OF DEATH

I already told you that we had shared the impending biopsy and then diagnosis with family and friends who were faithful prayer warriors. Somehow, word travels fast so mostly everyone knew what we were walking through. In sharing this however, I was not prepared for the darkness and very glum faces and the question "How are you"? Emphasis on the "you" as if I already had one foot in the grave. I am a pretty joy-filled and bright person the majority of the time. I have been nicknamed "Sunshine" at different times and continually radiate the Lord's love. These questions, while I know they were out of love, sucked the life force and joy out of me each time I heard them. The questions came before we shared that we did not believe we were supposed to go the "traditional" route of care. **Boy, when that cat was out of the bag, we were targets for all opinions**. Again, I know it was out of love and concern that people shared; nonetheless it was disheartening to be among so many believers that thought we erroneously heard from the Lord. It kind of reminded me when Peter argued with Jesus about His crucifixion.

Matthew 16:21-23 (NIV), *"From that time on Jesus began to explain to his disciples that he must go to Jerusalem and suffer many things at the hands of the elders, the chief priests and the teachers of the law, and that he must be killed and on the third day be raised to life. Peter took him aside and began to rebuke him.*

"Never, Lord!" he said. "This shall never happen to you!" Jesus turned and said to Peter, "Get behind me, Satan! You are a stumbling block to me; you do not have in mind the concerns of God, but merely human concerns."

I AM IN NO WAY SAYING MY JOURNEY IS THE SAME AS JESUS'! I AM SIMPLY TRYING TO MAKE A POINT THAT SOMETIMES WE KNOW THINGS IN OUR SPIRIT FROM GOD THAT OTHERS WILL NOT UNDERSTAND OR EMBRACE. THE OPINIONS OF OTHERS MAY BECOME A STUMBLING BLOCK IF WE LET DOUBT ENTER!

Jesus knew the journey He had to take, and nothing or no one was going to get in His way. I felt a similar conviction, I had seen very clearly my journey, and it was not a death wish but a life giving, faith-building walk ahead of me! A walk I was sure was supposed to be a journey shared with and by many! In fact, it was the Lord who commissioned me to write this book about this season and faith walk.

I remember sharing a bit of my frustration with someone who I felt would understand and not feel that I was being mean, but just needing to vent. This was immediately after I had been verbally assaulted by a naysayer who quite emphatically shared that I should not "play around" with my health. My confidant abruptly informed me that this is why she isolates herself and keeps her business to herself, so that no one knows what goes on in her life. She does not welcome the input. That hit me hard and heavy. How sad that this person was compelled to a life of isolation, walled off from the world, probably because of years of negativity from those who should be encouraging. In my spirit I instantly cried out for this precious person who missed out on sharing and rejoicing in the faith walks and testimonies that touch other's lives as well as our own. From that moment forward, I decided that no matter what someone said to me, I was going to pray and love them in spite of my pain, offering forgiveness in my soul, and standing unoffended. I was not going to hold back the "truth" of our journey or harbor any bitterness in my spirit! I was definitely not going to isolate myself. Isolation is a playground for the enemy! This story of walking through the fire of a "diagnosis of death" was one that I knew had to be shared for the Lord's GLORY to be revealed as a "declaration of life". I was going to count it as all joy no matter how painful!

Unspoken Words

With our decision to cancel the surgery consult came more waves of disapproval from those around us. It is funny how people can show their disapproval without ever saying a word. It reminds me of how our children get conditioned to our looks. I call it the "mean mom look". Moms do not have to say a word. We can stop our children in their tracks by one look. Not necessarily something I am proud of at times, but nonetheless it is true and it has proven useful.

One such time a precious prayer warrior friend told me that there was a need to talk to me and I probably would not like what was going to be said. Of course this was not unspoken exactly but I heard what the unspoken intention was. Now, I have to tell you that the Lord has grown me to a place where I realize that I do not have to accept or even listen to those things that may be offensive. The choice is mine/yours. Boundaries are both healthy and appropriate at different times. **<u>Victims have a hard time setting boundaries, but victors know the necessity of setting them!</u>** Of course, there is a distinction between boundaries and barriers. Many times barriers are erected to help us hide from things we need to face while boundaries set up strategies for appropriately addressing what is healthy and good. I do not believe that we should hide, scared of what we might hear, but there is a point where we need to draw the line. We need to accept truth and not be afraid to stand for our convictions. God continued to unfold Job's story into this journey. He reminded me that sometimes our closest and most beloved friends and family do not understand our calling or unique journey. I strongly believe that each person makes free will choices that determine consequences and outcomes. This conversation was one such choice.

This friend called me at the end of a very exhausting day. When the call came and the request was made to meet that night, I instantly knew that I was not in any place to be gracious and receive negativity. In as honoring and respectful of a way as I could, I shared that our meeting would have to take place when I was rested and full of the Lord. I also suggested that we both seek the Lord in this time for conversational direction. I was pressed to meet, but in the end, I stood firm, because deep in my spirit I knew the timing was not right! It was a boundary victory for the moment.

The next day I called on several prayer partners to pray for this impending meeting so that it would be a blessed time. A week had passed since I received the initial call. The morning of the meeting, Scott and I were sitting down to read the Bible together and my Bible flipped open to a page that I felt sure I should read. Having woken up a little discouraged and apprehensive about the meeting I knew that God was probably giving me a word that I would need to hear before the meeting. Mind you, at this point I did not have an appointment set up with this person, I just knew deep in my soul that tonight was the night! I put a marker in the place in my Bible and settled into the scripture that Scott and I were currently reading. We prayed after reading and Scott went off to eat breakfast and go to work. I took a deep breath, ready to embrace whatever the Lord had for me in that scripture. I turned to the section I had marked and dove in. Interestingly, the only thing marked on both pages where my Bible flipped open was this following scripture, highlighted.

Exodus 15:26 says "He said (the LORD), if you listen carefully to the voice of the Lord your God and do what is right in his eyes, if you pay attention to his commands and keep all his decrees, I will not bring on you any of the diseases I brought on the Egyptians, 'FOR I AM THE LORD WHO HEALS YOU'!

WOW, WOW, AND MORE WOW!!! Now I know this scripture was for a time passed but it was exactly what I needed to read! This could not have been timelier! Immediately my spirits were lifted and I felt as though I could face anything the day brought! This scripture remained with me all day! In the evening, I went to teach as usual on Wednesday nights. There is no greater joy than equipping children in Kingdom Culture and empowering them to pray in power for the Holy Spirit to heal through them! Wednesday nights were one of my truly sweet spots of the week!! After the class, as I had already sensed, my precious friend was sitting, perched on the edge of the seat, and waiting to talk with me. I said that Scott wanted to be there as well so I went and found him, and we all sat down to chat and pray. I have to admit that my insides were a nervous mess and my emotions were raw yet my spirit was at peace that this was the Lord's perfect timing.

I love how God answers prayers!!! First of all, there was no negativity not even a tiny speck entered into the room. The atmosphere was seasoned with His presence.

We briefly shared what the Lord had been showing us and our friend just asked if they could pray. The prayer was very soothing and healing. I felt the Holy Spirit encase the entire room. There was a peace and calming that something divine was happening in the spiritual realm. As my friend continued to pray, scripture started to be prayed. The prayer ended with.......OK WAIT FOR IT............WAIT FOR IT............... HAVE YOU FIGURED IT OUT YET?

Exodus 15:26 says "He said (the LORD), if you listen carefully to the voice of the Lord your God and do what is right in his eyes, if you pay attention to his commands and keep all his decrees, I will not bring on you any of the diseases I brought on the Egyptians, 'FOR I AM THE LORD WHO HEALS YOU'!

I almost fell off the chair! I had called Scott at work after I read the scripture in the morning. I shared the excitement with him that I once again felt confirmation in the healing so he knew just how profound this moment was! After our friend finished praying, we shared about what had happened that very morning with the same scripture! It was certainly a supernatural occurrence! The meeting, prayer, and scripture sealed in my heart what I had already known. I was being called to walk this faith walk no matter what the earthly outcome! God was in control and I was not going to waiver!

I would also like to share that this PRECIOUS WARRIOR friend faithfully continued to pray for me weekly, for several months past our meeting, sending me, via email, the prayers and scripture prayed! I truly believe that this amazing sacrifice and heart is one of the reasons that I walk in such confidence in the Lord. If you are a parent, friend, spouse, heck anyone, and the Lord calls you to pray for someone, let them know you are doing it and share the prayers, it will mean the world to them when discouragement or exhaustion hits! I look back and read these prayers when my mind starts to wander to dark places!

THANK YOU PRECIOUS FRIEND!!! YOU KNOW WHO YOU ARE!! I HOPE TO HONOR YOU WHILE NOT REVEALING YOUR IDENTITY!

Chapter 14

SERIOUSLY GOD

From this point forward I could feel that I was moving to another level and a shift in the atmosphere of my life. I walked with an even greater measure of faith than before. I no longer avoided those who were naysayers or death chasers. I walked with my head held high and shared my testimony of life with anyone who cared to listen. I was riding high on life. **THAT'S RIGHT, LIFE NOT DEATH!!!** It was amazing. That which could have left me feeling depressed and defeated had somehow become a life giving force for me!

I sensed the Lord was going to challenge me to even bigger heights. I was not sure what that meant but I could feel it coming. I woke up Wednesday, November 13th, 2013 with an incredible knowing in my spirit that I had to go resign from my staff position at my church as the children's director. I cannot say that this made me happy as things were going GREAT, at least from my human perspective!

I spent much time in prayer before going to the office. My conversation with the Lord went like this:

"Serio (Polish for "seriously", which I use quite often) God! Things are going great! The children are so excited about prayer and healing! Miracles are happening! Why now?"

His answer stung yet resonated as truth (of course), "That's right, things are great! It's not about you it's about me! You have been faithful and have done what I have asked! Your replacements are trained and ready. You did a great job equipping them. It is time!"

I had known the day would come. I never take on anything without equipping those around me to replace me. I have always believed in "working myself out of a job". Jesus was a great equipper and I really have wanted to model my life after Him since coming to know Him intimately, so I knew this was inevitable. I dragged myself into the office that day and was barely able to work, waiting for the moment to talk with my supervisor and give him my notice. He probably would not describe it like this, but we both cried like babies when I told him that I was giving my notice of resignation. Somehow though we both knew it was the way it was meant to be. After telling him, I felt much better. A huge weight was lifted off my shoulders that I did not even realize was there! I do not think I have ever enjoyed working with someone as much as my years working with him. We were a great team. The spirit just seemed to flow freely between us.

The next few days seemed to be endless. I had not been able to connect with our administrator to give her my notice. We had been through a lot over the past 3 years together and I really valued her friendship. I knew this would be hard for her as well. Finally on Sunday, I shared it with her. While all of us were sad, I believe that my "diagnosis" gave the blow a softening. It seemed as if this was almost expected. Looking back, I really see God's grace in giving me, what most of the people around me at the time would say was, an "understandable transition considering what we were facing". Yet in all truth, I felt it had nothing to do with why the Lord had plucked me out now. How like Him to make it a peaceable change!

Resignations and transitions in ministry, especially in churches, can be so hard. The body of Christ is a funny organism. This is similar to a family connected by Christ yet separated by walls. We construct denominational stockades that many times close us off from our brothers and sisters right down the street in another fortress. When someone is called out of one "church structure" and to another, there are many times hurt feelings that follow. I have heard it said that people tend to make up excuses or over spiritualize leaving one church to go to another, these judgements are not for others to make but between each person and God.

For me, I see it as the perpetual refining of the body of Christ. It is like the blood moving from the heart through the different arteries and veins. Rivers, streams, life is ever flowing, moving and changing, why do we try to dam up the body of Christ into a single dwelling? It is ever-moving and carrying regeneration to the body. It is imperative for a healthy body. The last thing I wanted to do was alienate any of my precious family at our particular church building! Yet I knew that my journey was going to not only take me off staff but into another "church building". My end date was set for December 15th, 2013. That gave us a month of transition time. This time seemed to be on fast forward. There were two things I recall from this last month in my position; one was in the church. It was my last day in the children's ministry which was PHENOMENAL. It included one of the most precious video testimonies from a lot of the children I taught through my three years there, great gifts, and of course lots of love. The farewell was, to me, as close to perfect as you can get. The other thing I remember vividly was our Thanksgiving journey back to Maryland to visit my family, which was two weeks before my last day.

Not A Mountaintop A Mall

We have made this journey every year for the last nine years. It had become our pilgrimage, pardon the pun. This was the first time my extended family would see me since the "diagnosis". They had heard our faith walk but had not laid eyes on me. I could feel the tension and relief as they saw me. Hugs were held longer. Statements of relief were shared.

When we started this pilgrimage, we decided as a family, to start going out Black Friday shopping. Our mission was to spread some love and cheer. There were always such horrible stories on the news of people being trampled, mistreated, and otherwise squished in the rush to "buy stuff". For me, this negated the very reason that the Christmas holiday season was adopted. While I know there may be disputes on the actual time that Jesus Christ was born, Christmas honors the MAGNIFICANT story of a God who loves us beyond anything humanly possible and gave us the ULTIMATE GIFT.

This year was a little different. Ever since I got connected with "treasure hunting", described in the same-titled book by Kevin Dedmon from Bethel Church, I have been hooked. Okay so if you do not know what "treasure hunting" is, let me enlighten you, at least to my way of thinking. First you pray and ask the Lord to give you clues as to who, what, or where He wants you to go and then you go and find the treasures (people) to pray with, possibly heal, and share about the love of Jesus. I encourage just going out and loving on people and praying with them but if you want to turn up the RISK FACTOR, do a treasure hunt!

On Thanksgiving night, my sister-in-law Kathy, and my nieces, Katie, Megan, Leah, my son Matt, and I decided to pray and ask God for clues for our Black Friday excursion. We prayed and asked for three clues each, not trying to limit God but using this as a teachable moment for my family who had not been on a treasure hunt before, well with the exception of Matt and me. As usual, God was faithful! We all got our clues; of course some got more than three! Some of the clues were purple and polka dots, long blond hair with dark hair under it, short brown hair, the Harford Mall, Harford, Maryland, etc… There were more clues but the ones that I mentioned were the ones that I am sharing in this story. We followed a lot of our clues but did not really feel like they were exactly what we were supposed to find. Finally we ended up at the mall. As we walked around, we found one store, a clothing store for young ladies that had purple and polka dots everywhere. It was TOTALLY OBVIOUS that this was our place.

We went inside and immediately I saw her. There in front of me was a young sales associate with long blonde hair with dark underneath. I went up and shared our story and asked if we could pray with her. She seemed pleasantly overwhelmed and said yes. I asked her if there was anything specific we could pray with her. She instantly shared that her mom was on dialysis and was dying. We all gathered around her and began to pray for healing. Tears spilled down her cheeks and ours as the spirit moved over her. I wish I could tell you that her mom was miraculously healed. The truth is I do not know what happened. All I know is that we were faithful to do what God asked and that everybody involved was blessed by this moment in time! It is so important not to think this is about me or you. It takes the pressure off and stops us from trying to control or alter what God is doing. We just have to be faithful and be who we are and let God be God. I could have asked for her phone number to follow up but I did not sense that was what the Holy Spirit was saying. Perhaps that beautiful young woman had prayed and asked God for a sign that He cared about her and we got to carry the message that she was a TREASURE and that Jesus loved her! Perhaps she went home and her mom was miraculously healed. **The beauty in trusting God is in understanding that I do not have to know what happened, I just have to be where He calls me** to be. I have always loved the idea of being a:

HUMAN BEING INSTEAD OF A HUMAN DOING. IF I AM DOING, THEN I AM PUTTING MY OWN WORKS INTO IT, WHILE IF I AM BEING I AM ALLOWING GOD TO MOVE ME!

Scripture is clear that faith without works is no faith at all. I believe that the "works" have to be the great movements of God on our life and then us responding in a beautiful synergy with the Holy Spirit. I want to share a prophetic word that a dear pastor spoke over my life; it's about striving. It has become a pillar of truth in my faith walk.

I was in a ministry meeting with several other leaders that I have grown to love. There was a speaker and some other leaders there that are highly regarded in the "power evangelism movement". I watched someone trying to talk with each of them. As I watched, I sensed the Lord showing me that this precious person's motivations were to get close to them and exalt them for personal gain. This greatly

disturbed me. As usual, when something disturbs me about someone else's behavior I look inward to see what God may be showing me in my own life. For me it is a way to always check myself to make sure that I am not judging others while doing the same. Kind of like "take the plank out of your own eye".

Matthew 7:4 says it like this, "How can you say to your brother, 'Let me take the speck out of your eye,' when all the time there is a plank in your own eye?"

As I began to pray for this precious person, asking the Lord to reveal to them that He is all they need to "get ahead" and pray for myself to see where this is showing up in me, the Lord gave me the word striving. He showed me that striving and pushing where He does not lead is sinful. I was both horrified and crushed. I have always tried to keep myself from putting others on a pedestal or from becoming a "groupie". This new revelation meant that I had been deceiving myself for years and worse, had been judging others! As I sat there, my body shook as if I was earth-quaking from somewhere deep within. The tears ran like a river from the deep roots of sin that the Lord was revealing and healing. I began to rebuke and repent of all the ways I strive in my life. I do not know how long I travailed there for both of us. By the time I regained my composure most of the people had left the meeting area. I arose, weakened but somehow refreshed. As I started up the aisle, my pastor friend literally jumped in the center of the aisle in front of me, pointed at me as if to admonish me, and yelled "Aurora"! Startled yet amused by his look of excitement, I jumped, yelled his name and assumed the same posture. He said, "I just had a powerful prophetic vision and word for you"! At this point, I figured, why not? I had just been through a virtual hell and back again from my uprooting of striving, so I said, "Ok, bring it on".... (I have to interject here, many times I hear very quick responses from the Lord when I pray and ask for things. However, I can honestly say that I have never had an experience quite like this one).

He kept pointing at me and said, "As you walked up the aisle, I saw doors flying open in front of you before you ever got to them! (His arms were flailing like doors swinging open) The Lord spoke to you loudly and clearly and said, "Aurora you will never have to STRIVE again, I will open the doors I want you to walk through and close the doors I do not want you to enter!" WOW, WOW, WOW! I was stunned. I did what any one would do, right? I burst into tears! What a confirmation and gift after minutes before coming from a place of brokenness and repentance! I have since prayed over this word and reminded myself about it whenever I felt myself trying to kick down or knock on doors instead of allowing Him to open them! I have also shared it with others for encouragement as I the Lord told me I would know who and when to share it.

I do not believe that this was a word to stop us from walking in faith and loving those around us. I believe it was strictly for when we are sinfully striving. Each of us knows when that is. If not, ask yourself this simple question – "What is my motivation here"? It is tell-tale. If you cannot answer this, quiet yourself before the Lord. He will always reveal our heart's motivation if we care to see. **Remember, hearing this from God is not always what we want to hear, but worth the pain to reach the peace.**

Chapter 15

IN THE MIDST OF THE STORM

Sometimes it is just plain easier than other times to quiet myself and hear God. Whenever I am equipping anyone, it seems to just flow. It is a reminder that when we serve others, we walk closely as Jesus walked. Why wouldn't we hear from God more clearly during those points? Sometimes, like in the midst of the storms of life, it takes great effort to hear or see God's movement. Not because He changes but because of the waves of attack that cause us to flounder beneath the water, caught in the undertow of the current, grabbing in panic for anything that may comfort us or help us to hang on to the last shred of hope. Shifting our eyes off the storm and onto Jesus is the BEST we can do in the midst of storms. My mom used to quote the old saying, "every cloud has a silver lining". There is so much scripture to support this. The problem is taking it from head (or academic) knowledge and embracing in the heart and walking it out with the Holy Spirit's guidance.

As I write this, we are coming up to the fourteenth anniversary of my mom's death. Since then, I have prayed and sat with many friends who have seen a loved one go home to Jesus. Each person handles death so differently and the grief that comes with it. For me, it was a time of complete transition in my life. So many waves were crashing I could hardly catch my breath. My mom's transition did not seem tragic to me. Somehow it seemed right. She had not been visibly or admittedly sick, except for the last month of her life, so it seemed sudden but in the depth of my soul I felt at least a year before this that I was going to lose my mom to illness. Perhaps it was easier to see my best friend (my mom) go home, because other swells from the storm of my life were hitting me so hard that I barely had time to recover from one to another. Perhaps it is just God's mercy and grace in my life. No matter what the reason for the relative ease and acceptance of her death, out of the other storms came one of the GREATEST blessings in my life.

My dad and mom were married until she died, which was forty plus years. In my dad's heart I believe they are still married. He worked hard our whole life growing up. He was always a steady force in the home, silently providing and unconditionally loving us. After leaving home at age nineteen, whenever I came home to visit or called to chat, my mom and I would spend most of our time together. After all, that's what best friends do. I had never really taken the time to get to know my dad. I knew he loved us and had been a wonderful supplier, strong and capable. I had just never really gotten to know him.

It was not long after my mom died that I had another huge life altering event that I needed to talk to my best friend about. I dialed my parents' number as usual, waiting to hear my mom's voice when the harsh reality struck and realized that the number was disconnected. The mechanic voice on the other end stated that I should check the number and dial again. It was not necessary, I knew the number by heart, and I still know it. It finally sunk in; she was not a phone call away any more. I did not know what to do. I needed to talk to someone that I trusted and could give me some clarity. While I had accepted Jesus as my Savior when I was fourteen, at this point in my life I still did not understand the peace from an intimate relationship with Him. So for the first time in my life, I called my dad, who was now living with my younger brother, Steve, my sis-in-law, Helain, and my nephew and niece, Steven and Krissa. It was to be the first call and conversation of many to come!! In this conversation, I found out that my dad prayed for all of us every day and spent time with Father God in scripture daily too. I never knew. I never took the time to stop and know before. It has been such an eye opening adventure and joy since my mom's death. The reason I am writing this, you ask? I found the silver lining in the midst of the storm. My dad is now one of my best friends. We love to shop, eat, and reminisce together! Just yesterday we spent several hours together which ended in a yummy lunch at the Green Turtle (my new favorite restaurant in Aberdeen, Maryland).

The silver lining goes along with the cup half-full or overflowing. Why settle for a half-full cup when God's store houses are overflowing with goodness for His children. I have not found any "apparent tragedy" in my life that God has not shown me the amazing blessing that has come from it. Though hard at the time, when I keep pressing into God, He is faithful to reveal the greater story. It took losing my mom, to find the treasure of a dad that was very much like God the Father. Strong, steady, loving unconditionally, provider, encourager, helper, always there and always willing to offer hope! Yet not willing to push himself where he was not welcomed or invited, desiring a willing relationship with his daughter.

Chapter 16

SEAL THE DEAL

After our trip to Maryland for Thanksgiving, time seemed to fly. Our DSSM class had finished just prior to the holiday, but the power of the experience lived on! I had two more vivid encounters with our healer in the form of open visions. The first was short yet impacted me greatly. It was a Sunday morning and I was at church worshipping the Lord.

It seemed as if I was in another world. There were people all around me. I was standing in the midst of all of them with beautiful praise and worship music playing, people dancing and singing. Suddenly, a golden goblet appeared over my head in the grip of a glowing hand. The goblet ever so gently began to tip and what looked like liquid gold began to pour all over my body. My first thought was that it was a spiritual oil anointing. Then the liquid began to be absorbed into my body and sear through my veins until every nerve, vessel, vein, and pathway was flowing with this golden light! Just as quickly as it appeared, it was gone! Stunned by the vision, I asked the Lord what the meaning was. I sensed that it was a vision of another part of my supernatural healing that was to come. This was yet another vision I would treasure in my heart and believe for the miracle.

This was now the third vision I had of my supernatural healing. We still did not feel any closer to making a choice in care to include alternative or traditional therapy. In prayer the only answers I got for treatment were, "Your body is my temple for the Holy Spirit, treat it as such" (paraphrased from 1 Corinthians 6:19-20! While scripturally this lined up, I knew there was more to this verse than just being able to quote it or eat healthy. I sensed that the Lord wanted me to go deeper with Him than I had ever gone before.

I began daily to ask the Lord what "treating my body as His temple" looked like in my life. I wanted to know how to go about this in my life. One thing I sensed was that there would be many, many people who would pray over me in the months to come. There had already been several churches I am connected with and prayer warriors from all over the world that had prayed for healing and continued to pray. I believed that God wanted the healing to be known through His hand alone. I believed that not one person, group, or treatment would be able to claim the fullness of this victory. It would be an act of God partnering with all the warriors crying out for me. I know that sounds funny, but I believe it is connected with the prophetic word about striving. Others would not be able to use my healing as a springboard for their ministry; the sole credit would go to Jesus!

Just prior to our Thanksgiving Maryland journey, a precious friend and sister in Christ, flew me out to

Colorado because she had heard from the Lord that I was supposed to come out for prayer with her and a precious brother in the faith! She and I connected nine years ago at the same church in Dayton as my friend in the ring story. It was also during the same Vacation Bible School. God used her family, and their pet guinea pig Speedy, to seal our friendship for life. Look for "Guinea Pig Prayers", a children's book about God's AMAZING POWER AND MIRACLES, we are working on, hopefully to be published soon after this book!

Anyway, in the course of this trip to Colorado, we also visited her wellness doctor. She shared many things with me and I shared my faith walk with her. My hope is that down the road, after this book is finished and I get verification of my healing, that ALL will read this and realize just HOW BIG AND REAL GOD IS!!

The one thing that really stood out to me was the fact that the liver was a filter for the body and needed to be healthy in order to eradicate cancer. She shared that many times people treat "the illness" like cancer or diabetes but do not heal the root, which she believed was an unhealthy liver that was not functioning properly. I am not a medical doctor so I am only sharing what she said. She told me that when I got back to Dayton I should find someone to help me walk through cleansing and healing my liver. It is one of the only things I remembered from her. In my heart, I knew I would not go back and find another doctor. At this point I was still fragile from the diagnosis and all the judgment from our faith walk. My countenance was still wobbly as I proceeded down this road. I needed more time to process and pray! This was barely a month after the confirmation and diagnosis.

It was such a beautiful visit and sweet time of prayer with my beloved Colorado family. I will always remember it as one of the brightest spots in this new journey I was called to! In the months from December 2013 to March 2014, besides a healthier, less sugar and carbs lifestyle, the only two things the Lord brought our way was alkaline ionized water and Young Living Essential Oils. While we now have adopted all three things into our lifestyle, healthy eating, alkaline ionized water, and Young Living Essential oils, I have never tried to "BE HEALED" through any of them. I have learned all kinds of information about cancer treatment, pH levels and energy levels and oil protocols, but I have not actively used any of these for the diagnosis. I have just implemented them into a healthier lifestyle. In the back of my mind is the word that I heard from the Lord that **"NO ONE OR NO THING WOULD BE ABLE TO BE ATTRIBUTED TO MY HEALING – JUST THE LORD'S MIRACULOUS HEALING POWER".** I did not take this word from Him lightly. If there comes a time that He calls me to a traditional or alternative treatment, we will do it, but for now, we are standing on the visions and promises.

In the beginning of December 2013, I had what will have been my final vision of my healing. I was actually sick in bed and decided to enjoy the time by meeting with God. I laid there and just marveled at the previous few months, my entire life, creation, the people I knew and still know and anything good from God, I lifted up praise to Him. As I rested and marveled at His goodness, I began to drift off into a light sleep. Suddenly, all three visions I had for my supernatural healing played through my head. Somewhere in the flurry of the visions I asked the Lord what He was showing me. He said that each were His SUPERNATURAL answer to the traditional treatments that we had decided not to pursue. The lion was the representation of surgery, the touch of Jesus and the explosion, the representation of radiation, and the liquid gold the representation of chemotherapy. He then told me again that I would be supernaturally healed to wait for it and trust Him! He said that this final vision was a confirmation and it "Sealed the Deal"!

Healing is such a funny thing. I do not mean the ha-ha kind but more of the interesting or fascinating kind. While everyone around me and I were waiting for the physical manifestation of healing, the Lord was growing me spiritually and emotionally. Furthermore He was using our family's faith walk to touch others. Each day brought a new strength of resolve and confidence in the power of the manifestation of the Holy Spirit than I had ever known before. My life was even fuller of His glory. As I once heard Bill Johnson say, "I want to leak the spirit" and I was well on my way!! I have such an intimate and close connection with my Abba Father and truly there is no place I would rather be than in His presence! I cannot explain the transformation other than I am an even **BIGGER** risk taker now and my heart overflows with love for all people! Okay, so you know there is another story that goes along with this "BIGGER"!

Chapter 17

CALIFORNIA HERE WE COME

Well to share a bigger risk we recently took, I have to tell you a story from about 25 years ago. Of course I was much younger then, not walking a very God honoring life, but none the less, still attuned to the voice of God in my life no matter how it showed up! I worked at a flower shop in Yuma, Arizona with a girl who was a few years younger than me. She and I were quite the dynamic duo! I really enjoyed her excitement for life, it mirrored my excitement. She was heading up to Sacramento for a visit. She asked if I wanted to come along. I loved California. I had spent many weekends driving over from Arizona, sitting on the cliffs in San Diego watching the sunset. How appropriate that they are called sunset cliffs. However, I had never been north of L.A.! This was going to be fun! We were also going to take a trip into San Francisco!

So, a few of us set out on a journey, across the desert on our way to Sacramento. The whole time we were in northern California, it was surreal, almost like living a dream. We headed back down south after a very fun-filled weekend. We were all tired and had agreed to share the driving. It currently was not my turn. As I sat in the back and watched the hills roll by, I started to doze off. Every time I shut my eyes, I could see headlights coming at us, it was night time, and then just as we crashed head-on with another car, I would jar awake. This happened several times before I sensed that I was supposed to drive at night. I told my friend what was happening and she agreed that I should drive during nightfall. We had decided to take the route along the Salton Sea to reduce the time in driving all the way to the coast and then over to Arizona.

By the time we started driving in the desert area of the Salton Sea, it was dark and I was driving. I remember seeing the stars more vibrant than ever and more numerous than the sand with which we were traveling along. They lit up the sky, which was comforting, since nothing else was lit up for as far as the eye could see. I do not know how long we had traveled.

Suddenly, I could see headlights racing towards us. The gap between our two vehicles was closing rapidly. I shook my head to make sure I was awake and not dreaming again. No such luck, I was smack dab in the middle of this very real experience. Everyone else was sleeping. Time seemed to escalate. The car appeared to be in the other lane so I took a breath not realizing I was holding it the whole time since seeing the car racing towards us.

I did not have even a split second to shout out to my passengers before the car swerved right in front of us, causing me to cringe! What happened next is again the kind of stuff movies and books are made of, which of course is why it is included here! I literally closed my eyes, prayed, and jerked the wheel to avoid the full frontal impact of the other vehicle. Remember, we were out in the middle of nowhere, traveling along the Salton Sea with sand and desert all around. The only other thing that lined the highway was electrical poles and there were plenty of them, which in the darkness I could not see.

I have to tell you, there is no way humanly possible that we did not collide with the other vehicle, as the car was right in front of me when it swerved! **THAT'S RIGHT, THERE WAS NO IMPACT, BUT WHAT HAPPENED NEXT WAS EVEN MORE AMAZING!**

As I swerved, the car lost control thanks to the plethora of sand on the road. I tried to correct the now out of control car. Suddenly from somewhere in the night I heard "Let go of the wheel". I didn't have time to think, I just listened to it. As the car soared into the night and desert, we hit a large bump and the car was launched into the air. A quick thought crossed my mind to throw my hands up in the air and shout as if I was on a roller coaster. Why not, I was already not holding on to the wheel. It was a split second thought and I was jarred back to the reality of the situation. As the car descended, I picked up my foot to slam on the breaks and stop the inevitable disaster. Just as my foot came down to hit the brake pedal, a hand gripped my foot and with great force held back my leg from completing the action. It was at this point that everyone in the car was awake and quite scared. It was also at this point that I realized I just need to "Let go and let God" or whatever angels He had sent to help through this situation. I did the absolute opposite of what any sane person would do; I relaxed and waited to see what would happen next. While these events seemed to happen in slow motion, I am quite sure that it was a matter of seconds before the car rolled to a stop, impact-free and upright on all fours but mechanically, DEAD.

It took all of us several minutes before we could speak or move. When I could finally open my mouth, I recounted the story to my very scared but blessed comrades. It was my friend's car and I felt really bad that it was not working. She however was very gracious and thankful that we were not all having this conversation in Heaven.

I am not sure how long it took for another vehicle to show up on the road. When one finally did, it was a trucker who stopped to help! He radioed for a police from the nearest town and waited with us until they arrived. Funny, I do not remember his name, I do not even know if I asked it but somehow I knew that he was an angel sent to help and comfort us in the darkness. I cannot even type this without tears of joy and thanksgiving for being alive to recount this and for there "being angels among us". I have always loved that song by Alabama, "I believe there are angels among us, sent down to us from somewhere up above. They come to you and me in our darkest hours to show us how to live, to teach us how to give, to guide us with the light of love"! I know I have been used as an angel in someone's life and I am sure you have too! However, on this night we were in need of angels and, poof, they were there!

The police finally arrived, looking around, with flashlights, to check out the scene. Before we could share anything, one of the officers flashed his light along the electrical pole that we missed by inches. He then flashed his light back to an embankment that we had to drive, or in our case, fly over to be parked where we now were. His questions and comments came at a rapid fire pace. I could not get a word in edge wise. His dialog followed pretty close to something like this,

"Why didn't you slam on the breaks when you hit that hill? It is a normal reaction. Your car would have flipped. Do you know how blessed you are? You didn't flip, you didn't hit the pole. There isn't a scratch on any of you. Do you realize that God was watching out for you? You should be dead. Do you realize that the car that almost hit you, hit another car down the road? The people were fine but the drunk driving the car was killed on impact."

When he finally stopped I could not utter a sound. Finally, the words came to all of us. We began sharing that we knew God was with us, so I recounted the whole story I just shared with you. The officer kept telling us over and over again how blessed we were. Needless to say, a friendship formed in the midst of a near death crisis, is a bond for life. That bond however would take a detour. My friend and I took different paths over the last 25 years that both of us would tell you were less than glamourous. Our paths lead us away from friendship and close proximity. The friendship that had formed amidst flowers and fire seemingly ended.

Now, of course, I would not have included this if it did not play into this new life journey! In the beginning of the New Year, we started praying about our summer mission trip. Our family or part of it has been going on mission trips or serving locally as missionaries, typically during the summer, since our union in 2005. In that time we took one vacation in 2007. It was a road trip out to the Grand Canyon and back, which none of us will ever forget. This year was no different. We were ready to find out where we would go serve this summer. We prayerfully asked the Lord where we should go, wondering what God wanted us to do this year. I will never forget the answer from the Lord, it was monumental and one that I would challenge you to consider with your own family. The words, "Your family is the mission"! "Take a vacation and enjoy THEM this year"!

I have to admit that the thought crossed my mind that maybe the Lord was making memories for us because He would be calling me home soon. The diagnosis hung in the air sometimes like stench from raw sewage. While I have God's visions and promises to encourage me, I still have that ever nagging voice trying to discourage me and cause me to falter in my faith walk! Nevertheless, it was a WOW moment – we love mission trips but always spend time doing and being with others during those times. While I do believe that mission work begins in the home, loving and caring for each other, it never occurred to me to actually take a journey from this perspective. I shared it with Scott, Matt, and Clint who were all agreeable. We chatted about where we would go. Finally we all decided that another trip out west would be fun, ending up in Colorado to visit our friends, that I spoke of earlier in the book.

We decided to set aside money from our income tax return and take the journey in May before summer vacations started and the parks and highways were crowded. I was really excited about this and a little nervous. Of course the enemy began to whisper things like, "God was not going to heal me" and "this was the last trip I would ever take with my family". I was determined that I would not listen to this malarkey. It took a lot of prayer, focus, and mental control to stop this present onslaught! Through great tears of grief I shared this with Scott. We prayed and knew that the enemy, the Liar was just trying to rock my faith and dampen our journey. It is so awesome to have Scott's steady strength and support in my life!

As the weeks rolled by, I began pricing rental cars, looking at camping spots, and detailing our journey. It was in the midst of planning that I again got a sense from the Lord about the trip. This time though, I really had to press in to make sure I was not putting my own desires into the plans. I sensed that I heard the Lord say that our family was supposed to go to Redding, California and visit Bethel Church. Now, I had been waiting to go there for years! I shared in my acknowledgment about the respect and honor I have for the leaders. I believed that one of the places I was supposed to go for prayer was there, so this was fantastic, but also a red flag, that I may be injecting my desires into God's plans. It took me some time and much prayer to believe that it was not just me, so I shared it with the family. They were actually all agreeable with the exception of Clint. He said he would go but didn't really want to; one of the main reasons was that it was too long of a drive. So we all prayed for God to show us the way. We decided that we would continue with plans for Bethel and if God showed us anything else we would be open to it. We knew we would have to alter plans and fly because Clint was correct, it would take too long to drive there and back. We would have very little time to spend there. Clint was still not convinced that we were supposed to go. So we continued to give it to God to decide.

It was during this time that Chuck Parry, the Pastor over Bethel's healing rooms, came to our spring session of DSSM class to speak. He was funny, joy-filled, and carried a powerful message of love and healing. Most importantly, he carried a message to Clint from the Lord. After hearing Chuck, Clint said that now he was really excited to go to Bethel and visit the healing rooms! This was awesome!! We took it as a DEFINITE sign from God that this was our destination. Anytime your sixteen year old wants to go visit healing rooms and spend time with the family is a time for great celebration! So many teens and parents are estranged. Many times Clint and I seem estranged to each other. Navigating parenthood in the best of circumstances is difficult, and we were facing some pretty tough things. I knew that while we all believed God, our own thoughts attacked us. I knew that Clint had spent some time worrying over me dying. It takes great work and huge faith, grace, and mercy to steer through the teen years successfully! Matt had traveled through those years but we still have a few to go with Clint! Prayer, love, grace, mercy, forgiveness, and communication are our key weapons of warfare in this battle!

So the trip was on! I could hardly believe that I was finally getting to go to Bethel and visit the healing rooms! However, I was hopeful that this would be the moment not dampen my spirits! I had waited to go and see the leadership and congregation "walk their talk"! I knew that I would not be disappointed. So where's the risk you ask? It's coming, WAIT FOR IT!

One day, in the middle of trying to finish a paper for school, I decided it was time to look up airline tickets. I was finishing my final class for my Master's degree in Counseling. Oh no, I can hear what you are thinking, this is sounding familiar. Just hang on because it is much different. I went on some of the discounted ticketing sites only to find out that tickets were going to cost us almost all the money we had put away. Again my mind reeled, "Did I hear wrong Lord? Are we not supposed to go to Redding? What should we do?" Somewhere in the middle of my brain overload, I heard the Lord say, "Buy the tickets." So, of course, I did what I do so often, I reasoned with Him. "We do not have the money for a rental car or lodging. Or for that matter, even food Lord!" Our conversation continued,

"Was I faithful with your Poland trip?"

"Yes, Lord!"

"Were you safe?"

"Yes, Lord!"

Here's where it got interesting. The response I heard, "That's right, you were safe! While you took a risk by going to the airport each day and praying for the money, you were still in your city and had the comfort of your friends and family around you! I am calling you all to a bigger risk with me this time! I want you to trust me to provide but I am requiring you to step out and buy the tickets before the provision has arrived!"

WOW – I totally understood this but still struggled with stepping out and taking action. I have walked with my ancient brothers and sisters as they had to take a leap of faith before things happened. For example, Moses had to take action before the Red Sea parted.

Exodus 14: 15-16 states, "Then the Lord said to Moses, "Why are you crying out to me? Tell the Israelites to move on. <u>Raise your staff and stretch out your hand over the sea to divide the water</u> so that the Israelites can go through the sea on dry ground."

While I realize this was no parting of the Red Sea moment, God was requiring us to step out in faith and take action first. By doing this, we were putting our faith into action!

Again, as He always does, the Lord ever so gently reminded me that He is the Great Provider and I did not need to worry. He is with me and will never forsake me! I knew I would have to share with Scott and the boys about this new development. I decided that there was nothing I could do about it at that moment. I had a paper due and nobody was home anyway. I returned to my paper and tried to put it out of my head.

I did a really good job of avoiding the conversation with the family for about a week. I wrestled with the Lord again and again about this. Of course, there was the constant nagging conviction in my head that I was walking in disobedience. We finally sat down and chatted. I shared about the ticket costs. I also shared that we may end up in the airport in Sacramento for 10 days praying and fasting. I told them I heard nothing past that we needed to purchase the tickets and that we were being called to a greater measure of faith. I am really sure that none of us believed that this journey would end in an airport in California for ten days hungry, un-showered, and wrecked, so everyone agreed that the tickets should be purchased.

I had already been having dialog with a couple in Redding, California who owned a home opened to people coming for a visit to Bethel. At the time they did not know us or anything about us. I shared that we were walking in faith about the entire trip. I shared my diagnosis and the course with which we felt the Lord was leading us. They agreed to continue to walk in faith with us and see what the Lord would do. I honestly thought that they would tell us to come and stay with them free of charge. What I did not realize at the time was that everyone that came to stay with them was on a journey of some sort of faith walk of healing with the Lord and they have a ministry to fund. Needless to say this was not what the Lord had in mind. I am getting ahead of myself.

As the weeks rolled by, I shared our testimony with several people and asked them to pray. There is one particular friend who was really discouraged overall in life. She was broke, tired, and hopeless. Our story encouraged her to trust the Lord and step out in faith in her own life. One day she walked up to me during our DSSM class and put an envelope in my hand that I could feel had coins and some type of dollars, hugged me and left. I put it in my bag until later in the evening. What really struck me though as she walked away was the voice I heard from the Lord saying that this was the "widow's offering". I went home and looked up the scripture and began to weep. I knew she and her husband had little money and that this was a sacrifice. The bigger blessing was to read how Jesus felt about her sacrifice, the "widow's sacrifice" in the Bible. The mere fact that Jesus highlighted the widow's gift of worship and sacrifice to the disciples is amazing. I wonder if she ever knew on earth the impact that her sacrifice would make on so many people throughout the centuries including mine and my friend's. I could hardly wait to share it with her. I wanted her to realize the HUGE spiritual impact she had just made in so many lives because I knew I would share this story with as many as I could. I included the scripture below for you to ponder and pray about.

Mark 12:41-44 (NIV) "Jesus sat down opposite the place where the offerings were put and watched the crowd putting their money into the temple treasury. Many rich people threw in large amounts. But a poor widow came and put in two very small copper coins, worth only a few cents. Calling his disciples to him, Jesus said, "Truly I tell you, this poor widow has put more into the treasury than all the others. They all gave out of their wealth; but she, out of her poverty, put in everything—all she had to live on."

There were other generous people who blessed us with financial offerings which gave us almost enough money for our lodging with our new friends in Redding. There was still the challenge of a vehicle, food, gas, and anything else. Now I already spilled the beans, let the cat out of the bag, or any other expression you want to use, that we went to Redding. What you will now see is the beautiful life journey; the tapestry that God has once again seamlessly stitched together. Okay this is now going to take a turn back in time again!

In the course of all of this, I remembered that my friend from long ago….. Remember the accident miracle? She lived in Sacramento, California. Thanks to Facebook, we had been connected through our old employer from Yuma, Arizona. She and I had not communicated much, just a few posts, nothing substantial. I thought since we would most likely be stuck in Sacramento for ten days, perhaps we could meet and reminisce. That would surely be a bright and sunny spot as we sat in our own stench at the airport. Okay, I know I am being melodramatic, but it did cross my mind that maybe this was God's plan. We had already bought the plane tickets and I was just continuing to believe that the Lord was going to provide what was necessary for us to make it to Redding! I contacted her to see if she would be interested in meeting. Below is our conversation off Facebook with my side comments, of course. I had not shared anything with her but we were coming.

Aurora Dubell Newton - 3/19, 11:50am

We are flying in to Sacramento on May 9th and will be heading to Redding in the morning. Our flight out of Sacramento is on May 20th. Is there any chance we could meet sometime the 19th? I would love to see you while we are there. My cell is ...... if you want to call to chat before we come.

Her Response - 4/8, 9:01pm

Aurora, when r u available on the 19th and when is ur flight out of Sac.? r u getting a rental car? Is all ur lodging already in place for ur whole trip or just part of it or what. Meals?

Aurora Dubell Newton - 4/10, 5:20pm

This trip is a long God story walk of faith... The short of it is that we bought plane tickets for all 4 of us because we truly believe God has called us to come out there for healing rooms and not sure what else. We used all our vacation money on tickets and are believing God for a miracle for the rest. I reserved rooms at a place called "in his wings" from the 10-17(check out) but have not paid yet because we just had a pay cut due to new insurance rates. Lol...my life has been a series of some of the most incredible faith journeys and this one is just a new level. I received a diagnosis of breast cancer in the fall. The Lord has shown me 4 visions of miraculous healing ... I have had prayer from all over the world and believe that this will be the final manifestation of the healing! So all that to say... I had to laugh when you asked very specifically about car...lodging...and food... All which we do not have yet. We have been laughing and making jokes about being stuck at the Sacramento airport praying for people and fasting for 10 days!!! I truly enjoy the risks and excitement of walking with Jesus!!!

Aurora Dubell Newton - 4/12, 10:41am

Realized after I sent this that you have probably not heard some of these adventures . Probably sounds a bit flaky but it's a great story. We fly in the 9th and will prob find a place near airport to spend the night. Right now plans are to go to Redding on the 10th... I would love to go to mt Shasta ...redwoods...ocean...sometime during our stay,... Check out is noon Saturday 17th... Thinking about heading to Sacramento and going to church there Sunday... Possibly Jesus culture church? Stay there until we fly out on the 20th am ... Kind of waiting to see what God wants to do with us during that time... No real definite plans

Her Response - 4/16, 5:16am

Aurora, don't know what all The Lord has planned for u, but if He brings u to it, He'll c ya thru it. Ur stepping out in faith and He will honor that. For me to get the word out and c what I might be able to get u help with, I need more info.

(First of all, can I just say that this is what real Christian family is all about? We have literally not talked in years. We both went very separate paths. We were both not seeking the Lord intimately after we crashed together all those years ago. Now, in the midst of our journey, she decides that she is going to help. She jumps right to business!)

Who all is coming? Two pairs I know, but what is the relation between pairs. Men or women on trip. Food likes and allergies. Can someone drive stick, has insurance? My hubby is trying hard to get u even a few minutes with either Bill, Bob or Kimberly Johnson.

Don't know much about Shasta, redwoods or other things closer to the seeding area. I'll def b able to help with sight seeing once ur in the sac. Area. U mentioned Placerville. It's changed a bit since u saw it. Lots of gold country all around though. Biblical gardens in grass valley is cool. I'm not familiar with the church u mentioned.

She Continued - 4/16, 5:34am

Possible day trips would be... Jackson, Jamestown, Tahoe. SF, Reno, Napa, Sonora, etc. things u can fit a few in a day, auburn, Folsom, Downtown Sac, Old Sac, Etc.

Aurora Dubell Newton - 4/16, 6:47am

WOW ...I really don't know what to say...I was just sharing a bit of the adventure with you! I am humbled by your heart! My number is .... if you want to call. My husband Scott and my sons Matt and Clint are coming. We are not picky eaters but try to eat healthy. Scott drives a stick... We are all insured. All you mentioned sounds awesome!!! Please call so we can chat!!

Aurora Dubell Newton - 4/16, 6:50am

Thank you for your heart to want to help!!! I am really looking forward to seeing you! I am so blessed to know Jesus has changed both of our lives!

The rest of the conversation was about our children and a bit of life information. Most of the trip information came in the way of phone. We had several calls and laughed and remembered a lot. It's funny how when you look back in life you can remember so much. For me, I had remembered all my sin and ugliness. She had a different perspective and shared some very treasured events that reminded me that even when I was not running after the Lord, God had my heart!

It was in one of our conversations that she informed me that they were lending us her Toyota Forerunner for the entire time. To put this in perspective…that is about a $700 savings right there! She also said that there would be groceries as well. Tears spilled from my eyes. WOW… I did not see this in the beginning of this adventure! I was speechless! I thanked her over and over again! It was all set; they were meeting us at the airport!

Our adventure was incredible. We spent a great deal of time at Bethel. We spent time in their prayer house (Alabaster House) which was my favorite thing to do. One of my troops hiked up there with me every morning so I could sit with the Lord and look at out at Mount Shasta. We also got to visit Mount Shasta which came loaded with a wild bobcat sitting and sunning himself waiting for me to snap a picture. We went to the redwoods which I have waited to see since I was a very little girl. We saw the ocean, hiked to a few different falls, went to San Francisco, Old Sacramento, met so many wonderful people, and spent time in the healing rooms. It is funny how the healing rooms seemed like the BIG part of the journey but now seemed like such a small part of why we were supposed to walk this out. What struck me the most about this entire trip was how the Lord had seamlessly orchestrated all of it into what I would conclude was the perfect vacation! In the midst of it, He reminded me that He created me for a purpose greater than I had been willing to accept for most of my life, not because I did not believe Him but because trials and tribulations had caused me to doubt I was worth anything. He took me back to when I was three years old, the true beginning of this ongoing journey.

Chapter 18

BEGINNING THIS ONGOING JOURNEY

During the third year of my life, I was diagnosed with a rare disease that was killing me. The diagnosis was a bowel blockage caused by the bite of a spider to which I was allergic. I needed an operation to remove over a foot of blockage. I remember being force-fed prune juice and a gooey paste that was supposed to be chocolate flavored to help move the blockage out of my body so that the dangerous surgery was not necessary. May I just add, **TOO BAD IT DID NOT RUIN THE TASTE OF CHOCOLATE FOR ME! I COULD USE DIVINE INTERVENTION FROM MY SWEET TOOTH** ☺ When the doctors realized that all of this was not working, it was decided that I would have to undergo surgery. Back then, surgery was not the cyber knife or laser experience of today. As a matter of fact, I sport a three inch scar just to the right of my belly button, as a rite of passage for my resurrected life. I think here is where my earthly ordinary, normal, or typical start became extraordinary and supernatural.

There were two doctors who were working together on my case. One was insistent that they operate immediately to remove the blockage. The other doctor believed that God would show him the exact time to perform the surgery, my mother told me all this, years later, and my dad confirmed her story. He was sure that anything done before or after that time would kill me.

The first doctor believed that I would die if they did not operate immediately. In the course of this debate, I was diagnosed with double pneumonia. While I do not understand all the medical things, this was described by my mom as walking pneumonia and regular pneumonia. My temperature was very high for days and there was no possible way for surgery to take place until it was back to normal. The first doctor still pressed for the immediate surgery.

While waiting for my fever to break, my parents tried to keep me in fresh air while at the same time protect my delicate condition. I remember laying out on our front porch in a chaise lounge, looking up to the sky and wondering about God. It was a simple child-like wonder but very memorable for me. I had a damp washcloth on my head to cool me down and a blanket wrapped around me to keep me warm. I could not move from being bundled so tightly. I wonder if that is how chicken feels wrapped up in a tortilla for a burrito.

Anyway, one night I looked up in the sky and there were squiggly lines and light creeping across. I started yelling for my parents, they ran out, alarmed by my shouts. I pointed to the lights and asked about them. With relief that something horrible had not happened, they told me that it was the northern lights, "the Aurora Borealis". They told me that it was a phenomenon that rarely appeared in the east coast sky of Maryland. This was the first time my mom had told me that it was named for the dawn or light and that was why it had my name in its title because, as I've already shared, my name means dawn or light. This was the first time my mom had told me that I was beautiful and that God told her that I would someday be a light in the world for Him, so that is why she named me Aurora. I just did not remember it as a distraught teen.

In the thought process of simple childlike reason, I remember thinking that the Aurora Borealis was not very pretty, just different. There were no pretty colors, just light and dark and squiggles. I wondered if I would be ugly but somehow people would see God's light in me and it would look pretty. It was a profound moment that I have thought about over the past decade. The million dollar question for me, **"Are we beautiful merely because we were created by a WONDERFUL GOD or are we beautiful when His light manifests through our lives"?** And then, what is beauty, really? My mom used to say that BEAUTY IS IN THE EYES OF THE BEHOLDER. This is why I might find a lily to be the most beautiful flower while you may think it would be a rose. Anyway…

Fast-forward, my fever broke and the first doctor was ready, with scalpel in hand, to begin the surgery. The second doctor was still standing firm that it was not time yet. My parents had a decision to make. I actually had a similar decision to make when Matt was a baby! He had a febrile seizure and went into convulsions. We called 911 and the medics came. In the ambulance an emergency room doctor gave directions for a medication to be administered to him. Something did not set right in my spirit. I asked the medics, whom I knew, to not administer it. When we arrived at the hospital, after check-in, it was confirmed that the direction was wrong and I could have lost my son. As parents, we really need to trust the leading of the Holy Spirit especially with our children. This really takes practice, to quiet all the other noise going on in our minds, to hear and discern the Lord's will for situations.

Not long before my mom died she shared that she believed that the second doctor was an angel that God had sent to save my life. My parents listened to the second doctor, "the angel" and waited. This book is a testimony to the fact that he was right. Now you may be thinking that the other doctor may have been right too, we will never know. I have found that questioning the AMAZING gifts given by God in life diminishes the testimony to the greatness of God's glory. I DO NOT QUESTION, I ACCEPT THEM AND REJOICE IN THEM.

Have you ever questioned something great and found yourself disbelieving in the miracle? I am challenging you to change your perspective. Use positive eyes to see the world and God's presence. My hope is that by taking the time to share in my adventure, you will find the positively AWESOME journey and testimony in your own life. Seek to discover the small, natural miracles that occur that make your life supernatural.

After my operation, I remember going to get my stitches out. I was hanging on to a stuffed zebra that someone had given me. I also remember wanting my dad to hold me while the doctor took out the stitches. There was a disappointment in my mom's eyes that I never forgot. I have often thought about that. Since becoming a parent and raising my boys, I realize that as a mom, we want to nurture our children, I had in the moment, robbed her of that. Please understand, I am not feeling bad about this, I was a little girl wanting her daddy to protect her, but I am ever seeking to uncover why people do the things they do. In my quest to love as best I can, it helps me to understand the depth with which people feel and think particularly concerning my interaction with them.

When I came home from my hospital stay for good, stitches gone, there was a joy and relief in my parents. I could sense they were different even though I was little. I also remember being very hungry and asking them for something to eat. They asked what I wanted. In my most grown up fashion I pronounced that I wanted a banana and a scooter pie. For those of you who may not have grown up in my era, a scooter pie is the same thing as a moon pie or a chocolate covered, soft sandwich or cookie with marshmallow in the center. I gobbled down my banana and then proceeded to gobble down the scooter pie. Not all good things fit well together. There is a time and place for everything including bananas and scooter pies. I remember that the two created the most horrible taste in my mouth. It was years before I could eat either one again. But the memory of the horrible taste kept alive the memory of the overwhelming relief that I was alive and there was something great going to happen in my life.

It was in this very dramatic episode of my life that I believe a divine connection with our Creator was forged which has led me to walk in the adventure of the mountaintop, mall, street, or wherever, taking risks, to love and live, a naturally supernatural life, to WAIT FOR IT!

Still Walking In Faith

So many amazing things have happened since I received the painful diagnosis just over a year and a half ago now. I have grown in ways that I never thought possible. I have learned to live more in the moment and less looking back. As I have faced losing my life, I found real life! I no longer fear the judgment of people, only God reserves the right as our judge. I have found that many people walk around with their eyes focused on the difficulty. I have witnessed people with whom I care for very much, living to die each day, consumed by illness, disease, bitterness, regret, the list goes on and on. It is easy to focus on the trials especially when pain, fear, and hopelessness grip you. It is in all of these things that I have found the strength through Jesus to awake each morning – "Dying to live". I am so excited to see what is around the next corner with Jesus that I do not have time to be distracted by anything else.

As I close this book, my prayer is that you will wake up each day and be "Dying to live, instead of living to die". Not allowing life circumstances to rob you of God's great for your life.

It's a choice no matter how hard. I hope you make the tough choice and WAIT FOR IT... the miracle to manifest and continue to WALK IN FAITH.

DECLARATIONS

I AM GOD'S…
- Possession (Genesis 17:8 / 1Corinthians 6:20)
- Child (John 1:12)
- Workmanship (Ephesians 2:10)
- Friend… (James 2:23)
- Temple (1 Corinthians 3:16)
- Vessel (2 Timothy 2:2)
- Co-laborer (1 Timothy 5:18)
- Witness (Acts 1:8)
- Soldier (2 Timothy 2:3)
- Ambassador (2 Corinthians) 5:20
- Minister/instrument (Acts 26:16 / 1Timothy 4:6)
- Chosen (Ephesians 1:4)
- Beloved (Romans 1:7 / 2 Thessalonians 2:13)
- Precious jewel … (Malachi 3:17)
- Heritage (1 Peter 5:3)

I HAVE BEEN…
- Redeemed by the blood (Revelation 5:9)
- Set free from sin /condemnation (Romans 8:1-2)
- Set free from Satan's control (Colossians 1:13)
- Set free from Satan's kingdom (Ephesians 2)
- Chosen before foundation of world(Ephesians 1:4)
- Predestined to be like Jesus (Ephesians 1:11)
- Forgiven of all my trespasses (Colossians 2:13)
- Washed in the blood of the Lamb (Revelation 1:5)
- Given a sound mind (2 Timothy 1:7)
- Given the Holy Spirit (2 Corinthians 1:22)
- Adopted into God's family (Romans 8:15)
- Justified freely by his grace (Romans 3:24)
- Given all things pertaining to life (2 Peter 1:3)
- Given great and precious promises (2 Peter 1:4)
- Given ministry of reconciliation (2Corinthian 1:22)

- Authority over the power of enemy (Luke 10:19)
- Given access to God (Ephesians 3:12)
- Given wisdom (Ephesians 1:8)

I AM…

- Complete in him (Colossians 2:10)
- Free forever from sin's power (Romans 6:14)
- Sanctified (1 Corinthians 6:11)
- Made for the Master's use (2 Timothy 2:21)
- Eternally kept in the palm of his hand (John 10:29)
- Kept from falling (Jude 1:24)
- Kept by the power of God (1 Peter 1:5)
- Not condemned (Romans 8:1-2)
- One with the Lord (1 Corinthians 6:17)
- On my way to heaven (John 14:6)
- Quickened by his mighty power (Ephesians 2:1)
- Seated in heavenly places (Ephesians 1:3)
- The head and not the tail (Deuteronomy 28:13)
- Light in the darkness (Matthew 5:14)
- Candle in a dark place (Matthew 5:15)
- A city set on a hill (Matthew 5:14)
- Salt of the earth (Matthew 5:13)
- His sheep (Psalm 23 / Psalms 100:3/ John 10:14)
- A citizen of heaven (1 Peter 2:11)
- Hidden with Christ in God (Psalms 32:7)
- Protected from the evil one (1 John 5:18)
- Secure in Christ (John 10:28-29)
- Set on a Rock (Psalms 40:2)
- More-than-a-conqueror (Romans 8:37)
- Born again (1 Peter 1:23)
- A victor (1 John 5:4)
- Healed by his stripes (Isaiah 53:6)
- Covered by the blood of Jesus (Revelation 12:11)
- Sheltered under his wing (Psalms 91:4)
- Hidden in secret place of Almighty (Psalms 91:1)

I HAVE...

- Access to the Father (Romans 5:2)
- A home in heaven waiting for me (John 14:1-2)
- All things in Christ (2 Corinthians 5:17)
- A living hope (1 Peter 1:3)
- An anchor to my soul (Hebrews 6:19)
- A hope that is sure and steadfast (Hebrews 6:19)
- Authority to tread on serpents (Luke 10:19)
- Power to witness (Acts 1:8)
- The tongue of the learned (Isaiah 50:4)
- The mind of Christ (1 Corinthians 2:16)
- Boldness and access (Hebrews 10:19)
- Peace with God (Romans 5:1)
- Faith as a grain of mustard seed (Luke 17:6)

I CAN...

- Do all things through Christ (Philippians 4:13)
- Find mercy and grace to help (Hebrews 4:16)
- Come boldly to the throne (Hebrews 4:16)
- Quench all the fiery darts (Ephesians 6:16)
- Tread on the serpent (Luke 10:19)
- Declare liberty to captives (Isaiah 61:1)
- Pray always and everywhere (Luke 21:36)
- Chase a thousand (Joshua 23:10)
- Defeat (overcome) the enemy (Revelation 12:11)
- Tread Satan under foot (Romans 16:20)

I CANNOT...

- Be separated from God's love (Rom 8:35-39)
- Perish or be lost (John 10:28 / John 3:16)
- Be moved (Psalms 16:8)
- Be taken out of my Father's hand (John 10:29)
- Be charged or accused (Romans 8:33)
- Be condemned (1 Corinthians 11:32)

About the artist/artwork on the cover:

 This is Marcella Roe; Princess (Daughter of God-Royal Heir), Wife, Mother, Grandmother, Pastor, Artist, and friend. Marcie's painting touched my life profoundly as it was the picture that was in my spirit more than 13 years ago when I truly found Jesus Christ. Some 10 years later she painted this picture and I saw it at a Women's Conference. Compelled to write this current journey of my life and moved by the picture that represents it, I asked Marcie if I could use it as my book cover. She blessed me with a digital copy so it could be used as the symbol of the freedom in waiting for it… the Lord to move in my life!

Her gift of prophetic art has touched many lives. Marcie mentors artists to be free to creatively express what God has placed in their hearts. It is her heart of releasing the kingdom through the arts that has empowered me to press on and complete this book! I pray there is a Marcie in your life releasing what God has ordained you for!!

90226541R00093

Made in the USA
Columbia, SC
28 February 2018